Rediscovering the

FOUNDING FATHERS

MORIN BISHOP

CENTENNIAL BOOKS

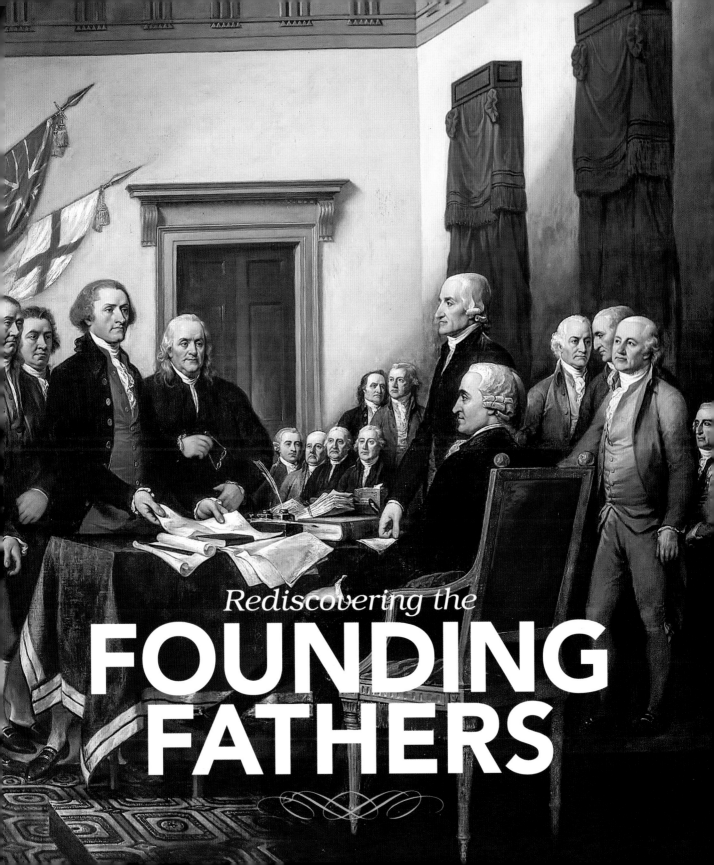

Rediscovering the
FOUNDING
FATHERS

CONTENTS

A Nation Is Born

HISTORIANS ARE IN AGREEMENT on the two seminal events that constitute the founding of the nation we know as the United States. The first was the revolt against British rule and the war for independence that flowed from it, and the second was the movement that led to the composition and passage of the U.S. Constitution, which defined the rules by which the new nation was—and continues to be—governed. In many ways the two developments were contradictory: The first was fundamentally disruptive, driven by intense hatred for an authority the colonists came to view as deeply illegitimate; the second was fundamentally constructive, motivated by a recognition among the young nation's most brilliant minds that a strong federal government was the only way to bind America's disparate parts into a single, unified whole.

But historians agree, these two divergent interests were each essential to the nation's founding: Without the elimination of British rule, no constitution would have been possible; without the Constitution, the war would have been in vain and America would have been plunged into a state of near-constant civil war.

And just how do we determine which "Founding Fathers" were most fundamental to the successful resolution of these two seminal events? Here it gets a bit tricky. To begin, there is a near-unanimity of support accorded to six men whose contributions to the country's establishment cannot be denied: George Washington, John Adams, Thomas Jefferson, Benjamin Franklin, Alexander Hamilton and James Madison.

George Washington was the charismatic leader of the fight, the general who defeated the British and then rallied the nation as the only unanimously elected president in U.S. history. John Adams was the indispensable figure in the years leading up to the Revolution, both publicly and behind the scenes, pushing the Continental Congress to sanction the drive for independence, organizing the resources to fight the war, and lobbying in private for the accommodations necessary to ensure support from both North and South. Thomas Jefferson belongs on the list, too, if only as the author of the Declaration of Independence and the sponsor of the Louisiana Purchase, which effectively doubled the size of his nation. Without Benjamin Franklin, the nation's most celebrated sage, and his brilliance in enlisting the aid of the French, the cause of independence would probably have been lost on the battlefield. And no one was more influential in defining the contours of the U.S. Constitution than James Madison, and no one was more critical to the ratification of that document or to the establishment of the federal government that resulted from it than Alexander Hamilton.

In addition, historians propose several other figures who played a vital role in the founding of the nascent nation and its groundbreaking system of democracy. Samuel Adams' leadership of the Sons of Liberty was critical to the growth of revolutionary fervor in Boston. John Jay, the erudite New Yorker, contributed to the influential *Federalist Papers* and was among the nation's earliest abolitionists. We've also included James Monroe, whose historic Monroe Doctrine laid the groundwork for the United States to operate as a fully free republic separate from colonial rule.

There are a few names not included here: Some historians make the case for John Marshall, the man most responsible for the establishment of the Supreme Court as one of the nation's most influential institutions. And renowned historian Joseph Ellis even proposes eccentric Aaron Burr, whose tempestuous nature engendered the duel that led to the death of Alexander Hamilton. But there can be no doubt that the men profiled on these pages all played a vital role in establishing the very principles of the country.

"We…solemnly…declare, That these United Colonies are, and of Right ought to be Free and Independent States…"
DECLARATION OF INDEPENDENCE

And yes, they are all men, and they are all white—America was an undeniably patriarchal culture in the 18th century and the blight of racism, most evident in the enslavement of African Americans and the extermination of Native Americans, permeated every element of society. But there was greatness in each of our Founding Fathers, and the ideals they proposed as fundamental to the nation they initiated would later be rallying points for those seeking to expand America's protections to a broader, more diverse swath of citizens.

The nation would struggle to overcome the divisions in evidence from its earliest days. But nearly 250 years later, the United States—messy, imperfect, but ever striving to answer the call of its better angels—remains as the world's oldest functioning democracy.
—*Morin Bishop*

Events That Forged a Country

The Founding Fathers did much to drive the action that led to American independence, but as with all significant figures in history, they often were forced to react to events outside their control as well. Here are the happenings that defined the context for the leaders who appear on the pages that follow.

Oct. 25, 1760 Britain's King George II dies. His grandson, George III, whose attitude toward the American colonists will influence the British response to insurrection in America, assumes the throne.

Oct. 7, 1763 The Royal Proclamation of 1763 sets a western boundary on the American colonies and establishes British governance over the territory ceded to Britain at the end of the French and Indian War.

April 5, 1764 The Sugar Act, which places a duty on imported molasses and rum, is passed by Parliament, ostensibly to provide revenue for the quartering and paying of British troops protecting the American colonists. Local merchants and importers object, but much of the public remains indifferent.

Sept. 1, 1764 The Currency Act is passed, which prohibits the colonists from issuing paper money. Resentment against the British begins to build among the colonists.

March 22, 1765 The Stamp Act imposes the first direct tax on Americans, requiring a duty on a host of printed products. Cries of "taxation without representation" are heard throughout Massachusetts and Virginia.

THE ENEMY
The much-hated King George III is greeted by British Admiral Richard Howe in 1794.

FREEDOM ASCENDS
Americans raise
a Liberty Pole in
New York City.

March 24, 1765 Parliament passes the Quartering Act, which requires colonists to provide food and shelter for British troops. The law is flouted throughout America.

1766 A Liberty Pole is erected in New York City in celebration of the repeal of the Stamp Act. Its removal by British troops and subsequent replacement by American protesters leads to several skirmishes.

June 29, 1767 The Townshend Acts, imposing duties on a wide variety of goods, are enacted, further fanning colonial resentment of British rule.

March 5, 1770 A confrontation between protesters and British troops leads to the Boston Massacre. Five Americans are killed.

May 10, 1773 Parliament passes the Tea Act, which mandates that colonists buy only tea exported by the troubled British East India Company, which is subject to a duty upon its delivery in America.

Dec. 16, 1773 A group of colonists, many of them dressed as Native Americans, board three ships in Boston Harbor and toss an entire shipment of tea from the British East India Company overboard in what would become known as the Boston Tea Party.

1774 Beginning on March 31, Parliament passes a series of measures, known as the Intolerable (or Coercive) Acts, in response to the Boston Tea Party. Boston Harbor is closed and Massachusetts is denied the right to local self-government. Americans throughout the colonies stage protests and the drive for independence takes on new force.

Sept. 5, 1774 The First Continental Congress is convened in Philadelphia to address American grievances against the British.

April 18, 1775 Paul Revere and his team of horsemen ride from Boston to Concord, warning Americans of the likely advance of British troops into their areas. Revere is captured in Lincoln, but Samuel Prescott succeeds in reaching Concord.

April 19, 1775 Fighting breaks out between American militiamen and British regulars in Lexington and Concord, signaling the beginning of the Revolutionary War. The war for independence would eventually last six years.

Jan. 10, 1776
Common Sense, a pamphlet written by Thomas Paine, is published, presenting an eloquent and persuasive argument for American independence.

The pamphlet is widely distributed and read publicly in taverns and other regular meeting places. Relative to the American population of 2.5 million at the time, *Common Sense* is still considered to be the bestselling printed product in U.S. history.

July 4, 1776 The Continental Congress approves the Declaration of Independence, which boldly sets forth American intentions to split from Great Britain and form its own nation.

March 1, 1781 The Articles of Confederation are ratified by all 13 states, establishing a new nation, consisting of largely independent states and a weak central government. Events in the years to come will prove the inadequacy of this arrangement.

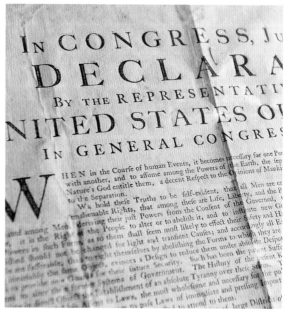

Oct. 19, 1781 British Lieutenant General Charles Cornwallis surrenders at Yorktown, effectively ending the fighting of the Revolutionary War.

Sept. 3, 1783 After 17 months of talks, the Treaty of Paris, negotiated with the British by John Adams, John Jay and Benjamin Franklin, officially concludes the war and sets forth the boundaries between the new nation of the United States and any remaining British territory in North America. The terms are highly favorable to the victorious Americans.

Aug. 1786–June 1787 Shay's Rebellion, an armed insurrection by subsistence farmers in western Massachusetts, is led by Daniel Shays and others who had fought in the Continental Army. The farmers suddenly found themselves deeply in debt, with some imprisoned for being unable to meet the demands of local merchants. The rebellion rages for nearly 10 months before being put down. The slow federal response, and the difficulty in raising the troops needed to meet the rebels, lead to calls for a stronger national government.

May 25, 1787 The Constitutional Convention begins in Philadelphia. Four months later, the delegates vote almost unanimously for a constitution distinguished by a sophisticated system of checks and balances, mostly conceived by James Madison. Of the original 55 delegates, only 41 were present to sign the proposed Constitution, and three (Virginia's George Mason and Edmund Randolph, and Massachusetts' Elbridge Gerry) refused to sign the document.

June 21, 1788 New Hampshire becomes the ninth state to ratify the U.S. Constitution, making it the official law of the land. The remaining four states will all ratify as well, though Rhode Island, the last to do so, will not ratify the Constitution until May 29, 1790.

April 30, 1789 George Washington, having been elected unanimously, takes the oath of office as the first president of the United States.

Dec. 15, 1791 The Bill of Rights, with its 10 seminal amendments to the Constitution, is ratified.

FINAL BATTLE
General Cornwallis
surrenders at Yorktown.

15

GEORGE WASHINGTON

The Leader

Washington was America's first—and utterly indispensable—national hero.

H E WAS NOT A GREAT ORATOR LIKE PATRICK Henry or a gifted thinker like James Madison. He could not write stirring prose like Thomas Jefferson or enduring maxims like Ben Franklin. But when the state electors gathered in 1789 to select America's first president, there was no question about whom they would select. They voted unanimously for George Washington.

The earliest years of Washington's life hardly suggested such an exalted outcome. His great-grandfather emigrated from England to Virginia in 1657 and the family apparently did reasonably well, though little is known about Washington's heritage before his father, Augustine, an enterprising sort who purchased considerable land and several mills, in addition to investing in the early stages of the iron industry. He was prosperous enough to send his eldest two sons by his first wife to England for their education, but by the time of George's birth to his second wife, Mary Ball, in 1732, circumstances had changed and George's education was largely informal. He attended school irregularly between the ages of 7 and 15 and received occasional tutoring from the local church sexton and a schoolteacher named Williams. Augustine died in 1743, when George was just 11, and his relationship with his domineering mother, troubled from the start, became even more full of conflict and disagreement. Fortunately, George's kindly, much older half brother Lawrence took over his care and George spent his adolescent years living, for the most part, with Lawrence and his gracious wife, Anne Fairfax Washington, at the home Lawrence built

DRESS FOR SUCCESS Washington fervently believed in the need for discipline and order within the ranks of the soldiers serving under him, which included having well-kept, clean uniforms. In his own case, this usually meant a blue wool coat with a "buff wool rise-and-fall collar," along with his cutlass and dress sword (above).

"Liberty, when it begins to take root, is a plant of rapid growth."

GEORGE WASHINGTON

ICONIC LANDMARK
Washington's beloved Mount Vernon plantation eventually consisted of 8,000 acres split into five separate farms, each with its own workforce, livestock and lodgings.

HOME SWEET HOME A depiction of George Washington at Mount Vernon during a hay harvest; lithograph after a painting by Junius Brutus Stearns.

on 2,500 acres blessed with marvelous views of the Potomac River. Lawrence named the estate Mount Vernon. Sadly for George, who came to view his half brother as a second dad—and a more loving one than his biological father—Lawrence died in 1752. His only child, Sarah, inherited Mount Vernon, but she died childless two years later. The property passed back to her mother, Anne, who by this time had remarried and leased the estate to George. Upon Anne's death in 1761, George became the outright owner of Mount Vernon.

By that time, George had proved himself adept as a land surveyor—he became the official surveyor

"However [political parties] may now and then answer popular ends, they are likely in the course of time and things to become potent engines by which cunning, ambitious and unprincipled men will be enabled to subvert the power of the people."

GEORGE WASHINGTON

THE FRIEND

George Mason

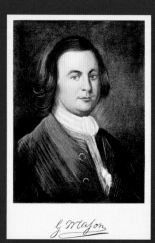

A neighbor and friend of George Washington, Thomas Jefferson described George Mason as "the wisest man of his generation" and viewed him as a mentor throughout his career. He held few official positions—he served in the Virginia House of Burgesses along with Washington and was a representative to the Constitutional Convention in 1787—but his influence on the principles that guided the nation's founding is undeniable. In 1776, he drafted the Virginia Declaration of Rights, one of the first documents to assert the fundamental doctrine of inalienable human rights—a theme that reappeared as a cornerstone of the Declaration of Independence, drafted later that year. Unusual for white men in Virginia, he was an opponent of slavery, describing it as "disgraceful to mankind" and resisting any compromise that enabled its continuance. At the Constitutional Convention, he argued for the specific protection of individual rights and opposed the final document—he was one of three delegates who refused to vote for it—as vesting excessive power in the hands of a central government at the expense of local governments and individual citizens. His views were highly influential in drafting and passing the Bill of Rights in 1791. He died the following year, possibly from pneumonia, at age 66.

for Culpepper County in 1749—in addition to learning as much as he could about agriculture and livestock management, two areas of expertise that would become central to his life after he took ownership of Mount Vernon. Over the next 20 years, Washington devoted much of his energy to the development of the estate, expanding it to 8,000 acres, carefully planting and rotating crops, and managing the 18 slaves that came along with it. Washington's views on slavery, evolving through the years, were overwhelmingly negative. He refused to sell his slaves for fear of breaking up families—"I am principled against this kind of traffic in the human species," he said—and he was renowned as an unusually benevolent master. In his will he directed that all his slaves should be freed after the death of his wife. (She chose to free them all in 1800, the year after George's death.)

Washington's marriage in 1759 to a wealthy widow, Martha Dandridge Custis, brought him additional funds, increased lands—some 15,000 acres—and, most important to his emotional health, two young stepchildren whom he loved with all his heart: John (known as Jacky) and Martha (Patsy), 6 and 4, respectively, at the time of the marriage. He would lavish attention on them both until, in what were surely the worst tragedies in a life filled with them, Patsy died in 1773 after years of what may have been epileptic seizures, and Jacky died, probably of typhus, soon after the British surrender at Yorktown in 1781. (For more on Martha Washington, see page 164).

INTO THE SPOTLIGHT

As much as Washington enjoyed his experience as father and farmer, he also showed an interest in a more public life from an early age. Intrigued by tales of glory recounted by Lawrence and other family members, he was determined to add military service to his rapidly growing résumé. He undertook his first assignment in 1753 at the age of 21. Virginia's Lieut. Gov. Robert Dinwiddie sent him—along with an interpreter, expert guide Christopher Gist, and four others, including two experienced traders with the local Native American tribes—on what was supposedly a diplomatic mission

to persuade the French to withdraw from disputed territory in the Ohio Valley claimed by Great Britain as its own. Despite difficult wintry conditions, Washington and his crew reached their destination safely—the French commander firmly rebuffed his overture, declaring, according to Washington, that "it was their absolute design to take possession of the Ohio, and by God they would do it"—but the return journey almost killed him. He was shot at by Indians, nearly drowned in the Allegheny River, and barely avoided freezing to death before making his way back to Williamsburg. But

MAKING PLANS With panoramic views of the Potomac River in the background, Washington reviewed plans for Capitol construction with his step-grandchildren George (left) and Nelly Custis (middle), his wife, Martha (right), and a slave, perhaps William Lee or Christopher Sheels (far right).

his courage in the face of these tribulations impressed his superiors, and over the course of the following five years, during what came to be called the French and Indian War, he would prove his mettle again and again, most notably in the British defeat at Fort

"Discipline is the soul
of an army. It makes
small numbers formidable;
procures success to the
weak and esteem to all."

GEORGE WASHINGTON

Duquesne (in present-day Pittsburgh) in July 1755. His mentor, General Edward Braddock, was killed during the encounter, and Washington himself had two horses shot out from under him and four bullets pass through his clothing without injuring him. His exceptional bravery and disregard for his own safety enabled the British to retreat successfully. It was also during these years that Washington developed a skill for bold surprise attacks, a tactic that would produce some of his most notable victories during the Revolutionary War.

In 1758, he was elected to Virginia's House of Burgesses—the body sanctioned by the British to represent the colonials—but in the years to come, like his fellow Founding Fathers, he came to resent the increasingly oppressive hand of British rule. He was in attendance for Patrick Henry's stirring introduction of resolutions opposing the Stamp Act in 1765, and when Virginia chose its seven delegates to the First Continental Congress in 1774, Washington was selected. Like most Americans at the time, he still did not consider

SAD DEFEAT The early days of the Revolutionary War produced a number of discouraging developments, including the occupation of New York City by Gen. William Howe's combined force of British and Hessian troops, who marched into the city in September 1776.

"Experience teaches us that it is much easier to prevent an enemy from posting themselves than it is to dislodge them after they have got possession."

GEORGE WASHINGTON

independence as a likely solution, but he had become more radical than most in his view of British intransigence. While others continued to hold out hope for diplomatic initiatives, Washington was convinced that sterner action (even if commercial), as opposed to military warfare, was the preferred course. "Shall we after this whine and cry for relief," he wrote, "when we

FIGHTING BEGINS A recruiting poster (above) urged all "able bodied and well disposed" young men to join Washington's Continental Army; the poster also included basic instructions on how to cock, prime, charge and fire a rifle. A map (right) by Frenchman Louis Denis illustrated the basic shape of the American territories at the time of the Revolutionary War.

CARTE
THEATRE DE LA GUERRE PRESENTE
EN AMERIQUE
Dressée
d'après les Nouvelles Cartes Anglaises.
par L. DENIS
Géographe et Auteur du Conducteur Français
DEDIÉE et PRESENTÉE
A MONSIEUR LE NOIR
Conseiller d'Etat, Lieutenant général de Police &c.
Par son très humble Serviteur
BASSET
en 1779.

have already tried it in vain?" When events in Boston escalated to the point of open rebellion and increased demands for independence, Washington declared his readiness to fight if need be. "I will raise 1,000 men," he declared, "subsist them at my own expense, and march myself at their head for the relief of Boston."

Soon after armed conflict broke out in Lexington and Concord in April 1775, Washington was named the commander in chief of all the American forces. The brilliance of this choice was only clear in retrospect, although John Adams—Washington's most influential supporter for the post—saw in the imposing figure of Washington a man possessed not only of exceptional leadership skills but also a figure whose Virginian heritage and outspoken support for the patriots in Massachusetts made him an ideal commander to unify North and South in the fight against the British. (Washington was exceptionally tall for the era at 6-foot-2, and muscular, with steely gray-blue eyes. A military aide noted that "his movements and gestures are graceful, his walk majestic, and he is a splendid horseman.")

HIS NATION'S SAVIOR

On July 3, 1775, Washington famously rode to Cambridge Common and, with sword held high, took charge of the Boston militia, quickly imposing strict discipline on all the men under his command. Washington was not a great tactician in the beginning; in fact, he committed a number of strategic blunders during the war, although some historians believe his greatest weakness was his tendency to heed the advice of his cautious subordinates too often instead of trusting his own instincts, which tended to favor bolder strokes. But like all of history's greatest military leaders, Washington was also highly charismatic, with a natural leader's innate capacity to command respect and loyalty from his men. From start to finish, through six years of intense conflict, including a famously brutal winter in Valley Forge, he held his forces together and drove them to eventual victory.

His two greatest triumphs came at very different moments in the war. The first was in late 1776, at the

AN UNFORGETTABLE IMAGE
Emmanuel Gottlieb Leutze's iconic depiction of Washington crossing the Delaware wasn't fully accurate—the crossing took place at night, with little available light; it was snowing; and it is unlikely that Washington would have been able to stand amid the turbulent waters.

lowest point for the American forces, after Washington had suffered a series of defeats and been forced to retreat from Manhattan northward and then westward across the Hudson River to the Delaware. Much of his force had been captured; others had melted away during the lengthy retreat; and much of the British leadership had concluded that the American insurrection was over. Desperate times produced the brashest action of the war: During a blinding

snowstorm, Washington and 2,400 troops—many of them fishermen and sailors from Marblehead, Massachusetts—crossed the Delaware River, marched 10 miles to Trenton, and caught the British troops there completely unprepared. Without a single casualty on the American side, Washington captured 1,000 Hessian and British soldiers, along with all their arms and ammunition. British Gen. Charles Cornwallis immediately marched his 8,000 troops to Trenton, but before he could engage his enemy, Washington and his men sneaked out of town—leaving campfires burning to fool the British—and headed to Princeton, where the Americans gained another victory over the British troops encamped there. The twin victories buoyed the American cause, produced a flood of recruits, and enhanced the standing of the Americans overseas—most notably in France, where an alliance, cemented in 1778, led to crucial aid.

Washington's other great triumph took place in the fall of 1781, when he brilliantly maneuvered his troops to outflank and force the surrender of Cornwallis at Yorktown, effectively bringing the war to an end. The victory offered proof that Washington, who began the war with no experience in the management of massive troop movements, had learned his lessons well and become a successful general in every sense of the term.

PRESIDENT WASHINGTON

Washington's contributions did not end with the war. Other founders played a larger role in the second key element of America's establishment—its brilliant Constitution—but Washington presided over the Constitutional Convention in 1787 and his staunch support was critical to the ratification of the Constitution by the state of Virginia. During his presidency, he set a number of precedents, including the establishment of a cabinet to guide his policy choices and a trend

GEORGE VICTORIOUS Soon after the British evacuated New York City for good in November 1783, Washington led his Continental Army from their headquarters north of the city into Manhattan (above) and down to the Battery at the island's southern tip. He and his men were greeted with wild acclaim throughout their journey. A year later, Washington posed for a portrait (right) by Charles Wilson Peale. He hoped to retire to a quiet life of repose in Mount Vernon, but the nation was not done with him.

toward a strong central government most eloquently advocated by the secretary of the treasury, Alexander Hamilton. But his greatest legacy, besides his pivotal role in defeating the British, was his decision not to seek a third term in 1796, setting up the nation's first successful transfer of power when John Adams succeeded him. The nation mourned his death in 1799 as they might have done the loss of a beloved king, but few were more responsible for the nation's dedication to democracy than he was. ★

"I hold the maxim
no less applicable
to public than to
private affairs,
that honesty
is the best policy."
GEORGE
WASHINGTON

America's Statement of Purpose

Richard Henry Lee of Virginia, little-known and remembered but for this single dramatic act, rose to his feet on June 7, 1776, to address the Continental Congress in Philadelphia and present three resolutions: First, "that these United Colonies are, and of right ought to be, free and independent States"; second, "that they are absolved from all allegiance to the British Crown"; and third, "that all political connection between them and the State of Great Britain is, and ought to be, totally dissolved."

The Virginia convention had authorized Lee to offer the resolutions, and in some ways they reflected the numerous acts of independence that had already been undertaken—the Continental Congress had instructed the colonies in May that they should form their own governments and "totally suppress" the authority of the British crown. But considerable opposition remained to a complete break from the mother country, particularly among the middle states of New York and Pennsylvania. Hoping to bring the laggards along, Congress decided to delay the vote on Lee's resolutions for a few weeks and appoint three committees to consider vital matters in the interim, including one group that was given the task of composing an official declaration of independence.

MISSION STATEMENT The famous painting (right) by John Trumbull depicts the moment on July 2, 1776, when the five-man drafting committee presented the first version of the Declaration of Independence to the Continental Congress for its approval. The document (opposite page), though passed on July 4, would not be signed until Aug. 2. "We must all hang together," John Hancock noted. "Yes, we must indeed all hang together," Ben Franklin famously replied, "or most assuredly we shall all hang separately."

The drafting committee was composed of five highly influential members of the revolutionary generation: Roger Sherman of Connecticut, Robert Livingston of New York, Benjamin Franklin of Pennsylvania, John Adams of Massachusetts and Thomas Jefferson of Virginia. Livingston and Sherman had other pressing duties, and Franklin was in almost constant pain from gout, leaving Jefferson and Adams as the two most likely contributors. Jefferson was well-schooled in moral philosophy and known to be a graceful and elegant writer, and Adams urged the committee to make him the primary author, not only because of his skills for the task but also because Adams knew how important it would be for Virginia to support the resulting draft.

In CONGRESS, July 4, 1776

The unanimous Declaration of the thirteen united States of America.

(In typically self-deprecating style, Adams also declared himself out of the running due to being "obnoxious, suspected and unpopular.")

Franklin and Adams reviewed Jefferson's first draft and made a few minor, largely semantic changes, before the document was presented to the Continental Congress on July 2. Much to Jefferson's consternation, Congress condensed and deleted portions of the latter part of Jefferson's declaration, which enumerated a host of colonial complaints in somewhat legalistic terms, but the soaring language that began the document remained untouched:

When in the Course of human events it becomes necessary for one people to dissolve the political bands which have connected them with another and to assume among the powers of the earth, the separate and equal station to which the Laws of Nature and of Nature's God entitle them, a decent respect to the opinions of mankind requires that they should declare the causes which impel them to the separation.

"We hold these truths to be self-evident, that all men are created equal, that they are endowed by their Creator with certain unalienable Rights, that among these are Life, Liberty and the pursuit of Happiness. That to secure these rights, Governments are instituted among Men, deriving their just powers from the consent of the governed..."

Congress endorsed this sweeping declaration of natural rights—although not a fully accepted principle at the time—on July 4, and a Philadelphia print shop quickly produced broadsides that were distributed throughout the colonies. On July 6, the declaration was read publicly to great celebration in New York City, where Washington and his troops were quartered. On August 2, the document was signed by members of the Continental Congress, some of whom had not been present in July to vote for it. Their 56 names— and the oversize signature of John Hancock, the president of the Continental Congress—would go down in American history as visible markers of the nation's first steps toward independence.

THE ROOM WHERE IT HAPPENED
The site of the historic signing in Philadelphia is fully preserved, including its original chairs and desks, in what is now known as Independence Hall.

"There is something very unnatural and odious in a government a thousand leagues off."

JOHN ADAMS

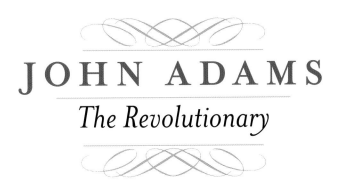

JOHN ADAMS
The Revolutionary

He wrote, organized and made speeches:
In the 1760s and '70s, Adams was everywhere.

TUBBORN, OPINIONATED, FULL OF FIGHT—JOHN ADAMS was surely one of the more difficult personalities in the American pantheon. When his strong principles and keen intellect led him to a conclusion, he stuck to it regardless of the consequences to his popularity or political standing. Sometimes he was wrong, but far more often than not he was right, and his dogged refusal to compromise his beliefs was critical to the formation of the new nation to which he was so devoted. Particularly in the years leading up to revolution, Adams' influence could be seen almost everywhere.

Born in 1735 to a family with roots in the earliest Puritan settlements in Massachusetts, Adams attended Harvard University in fulfillment of his father's wish that he become a clergyman. But young John, fiercely independent from the beginning, rejected the expected path and went into law instead. In 1758 he moved back to his hometown of Braintree—now Quincy—Massachusetts, and began practicing law in nearby Boston. Six years later he made perhaps the best decision of his life when he married Abigail Smith, a minister's daughter who was every bit his intellectual equal and possessed of opinions just as vehement as his own. The correspondence between the two, who were often separated by John's duties in Europe, stretched over 39 years, encompassed a total of more than 1,100 letters, and offered a portrait of one of the strongest marriages in American political history. Abigail eventually bore John three sons and two daughters in addition to a stillborn child in 1777. (For more on Abigail Adams, see page 168.) John was a critical and demanding father—he was just as

AN EARLY OUTRAGE The Stamp Act, enacted in 1765, levied the first direct taxes on British colonial subjects, who were forced to pay a duty on almost all printed products, which required a page bearing an official "stamp" (above), indicating that the tax had been paid. Adams (opposite) was a vehement opponent of the act.

tough on himself—and Charles and Thomas, his two younger sons, did not handle their father's demands, or his absences, well. Both later died from alcoholism, Charles at the age of 30. Daughter Susanna died from a childhood disease, perhaps smallpox, at the age of just 2. His eldest son, John Quincy, of course, though perhaps the most irascible politician in American history, fulfilled the highest hopes any parent could have, attaining the presidency in 1825.

LEADING THE REVOLT

Even in his earliest days with Abigail on the farm in Braintree, Adams was ambitious, longing to play a prominent role in the important issues of the day. "I never shall shine," he wrote, " 'till some animating occasion calls forth all my powers." Britain's increasingly oppressive grip on the colonies offered Adams precisely the animating occasion he needed to make his mark, and he became one of the earliest and most

The TORY'S Day of JUDGMENT.

E. Tisdale del.   et sculpt.

A RESTIVE POPULATION
Opposition to the Stamp Act led to numerous acts of sabotage and political violence, such as the stringing up of tax agents (left); a second agent at the base of the pole appears about to be tarred and feathered. As the violence escalated, British authorities were forced to provide armed escorts for wagons (opposite page) carrying the officially stamped paper to be used in printed materials.

A VIEW OF PART OF THE TOWN OF BOSTON I...

BRITISH REINFORCEMENTS
This engraving by Paul Revere depicts the arrival of a multitude of British warships and troops in Boston Harbor in response to Americans' refusal to pay the duties imposed on a variety of goods by the Townshend Acts in 1768. The accompanying text notes that "the Ships of War, armed Schooners, Transports &c Came up the Harbor and Anchored round the town... as for a regular Siege... there Formed and Marched with insolent Parade, Drums beating, Fifes playing and Colors flying up King Street Each Soldier having received 16 rounds of Powder and Ball."

ENGLAND AND BRITTISH SHIPS OF WAR LANDING THEIR TROOPS 1768

FANNING THE FLAMES A chunk of ice thrown by a protester that knocked down a British soldier may have been the catalyst for what became known as the Boston Massacre, which took place in front of Boston's Old State House (above). Paul Revere's engraving (right), which inaccurately presented the attack as fully coordinated, further aroused resentment against the British among the colonists.

eloquent voices of rebellion. In 1765, he wrote "A Dissertation on the Canon and Feudal Law" in opposition to the Stamp Act, the British attempt to levy taxes on virtually all printed paper products in the colonies. It was the first internal tax imposed directly on British subjects in the New World, and Adams considered it an egregious and illegal example of British overreach, as well as an illustration of British corruption in its attempt to squeeze revenue from the colonists to shore up England's failing finances. The Townshend

BUTCHER'S HALL

CUSTOMHOUSE

THE FIREBRAND

Patrick Henry

As one of his nation's truly brilliant—and stirring—orators, Patrick Henry made his mark in full public view. After some less-than-successful youthful forays into farming and shopkeeping, Henry found his proper niche and became one of Virginia's most successful lawyers, famed for his quick mind and even quicker wit in the courtroom.

Elected to the Virginia House of Burgesses in 1765, he quickly established himself as a powerful voice of dissent against Britain's oppressive policies. That same year, he introduced a series of resolutions in opposition to the Stamp Act, declaring, "Caesar had his Brutus, Charles the First his Cromwell, and George III may profit by their example. If this be

treason, make the most of it." His speech was greeted by howls of outrage from the gallery and some of his fellow representatives, who were not yet ready to split so openly with the British. Yet copies of his words were printed and distributed throughout the colonies, fostering a growing movement against the British rule.

Henry was selected to serve as a delegate at the Continental Congress in Philadelphia in 1774, where he met Samuel Adams. Together, the two helped stir support for revolution. "The distinctions between Virginians, Pennsylvanians, New Yorkers and New Englanders, are no more. I am not a Virginian, but an American," he declared.

The following year, Henry delivered his most famous speech, at the Virginia Convention on March 23, 1775. There, he defended his resolutions to prepare the Virginia militia to fight the British if it became necessary to do so. "I know not what course others may take," he thundered, "but as for me, give me liberty or give me death."

After the war, Henry became commander in chief of Virginia's troops, but he resigned after six months, helping to write the state's constitution in 1776. He later became Virginia's first governor.

A strong proponent of states' rights over a strong federal government, he opposed the drafting of the Constitution and called its principles "dangerous." Henry later played a key role in pushing for the passage of a Bill of Rights. The result did not go as far as he wished but did enable him to overcome much of his earlier opposition to the Constitution. "Show me that age and country," he declared in 1788 in support of the protection of individual freedom, "where the rights and liberties of the people were placed on the sole chance of their rulers being good men without a consequent loss of liberty!" Liberty—for himself and his fellow citizens—would remain his watchword throughout his life.

After leaving public service in 1790, Henry returned to his law practice and his family, fathering 17 children between two marriages (his first wife died in 1775). In this time, he turned down prestigious appointments such as attorney general, secretary of state and Supreme Court justice. Although he was persuaded to run for a seat in the Virginia legislature in 1799, he died before being able to serve—but his powerful words for the cause of freedom have lived on through the centuries.

Acts that followed in 1767, which imposed taxes on a variety of other goods, including glass, lead, paint, paper and—most famously—tea, aroused his ire even further as increasing numbers of his fellow colonists looked to Adams to express their outrage.

Three years later, on March 5, 1770—as colonial opposition to the British was reaching a fever pitch— a crowd of disgruntled Americans confronted a squad of British soldiers in an event that would be immortalized as the Boston Massacre. Disturbed by the heckling and fearing for their lives, the soldiers fired on the group, killing three men and wounding two others who later died. Angry colonists demanded that the soldiers be prosecuted for their actions, but who would defend them? Ever a man of conscience and eager to prove the impartiality of the colonial courts, Adams took the case, eventually winning acquittals for six of the eight British soldiers charged. "Facts are stubborn things," Adams told the jury, "and whatever may be our wishes, our inclinations, or the dictates of our passions, they cannot alter the state of facts and evidence." Adams was vilified for his actions, but as in so many of the controversies that would surround him throughout his life, he would not compromise a fundamental principle, in this case the right of every accused individual to a competent defense.

Adams' influence on the American experiment may have been most profound in the years immediately before the Declaration of Independence in 1776. In the summer of 1774, representatives from 12 of the 13 original colonies gathered in Philadelphia for the First Continental Congress. Adams was there as part of the Massachusetts delegation and he quickly established himself as among the most radical representatives, arguing not only that Britain had no right to impose taxes on the colonists, but also no right to impose any form of legislation on the colonies whatsoever. While some delegates hoped for reconciliation with their British overlords, Adams saw little chance for such an outcome. The logic of his position seemed to lead to only one destination: full independence. It is not surprising that by the time of the Second Continental

FAB FIVE
Adams, along with Benjamin Franklin, Thomas Jefferson, Roger Sherman and Robert Livingston, helped draft the Declaration of Independence.

Congress in the following year, he had become known as "The Atlas of Independence."

ACTIVE AND INFLUENTIAL
In the seminal 1775–1776 period, Adams took several steps that would have justified his selection as a Founding Father all on their own. First, partially in order to guarantee Virginia's support for independence, he nominated George Washington to lead the rapidly forming Continental Army and drafted

"The destruction of the tea is so bold, so daring, so intrepid and so inflexible, and it must have so important consequences and so lasting that I can't but consider it an epoch in history."

JOHN ADAMS

Thomas Jefferson to become the primary writer of the Declaration of Independence. Then, during the Congressional debate about the Declaration, he urged unanimous adoption of Jefferson's draft, arguing forcefully for a definitive statement of separation from British rule. Finally, after writing the document that operated as the framework for a critical treaty with France, he agreed to lead the Board of War and Ordnance, almost single-handedly taking on the task of raising and supplying America's first army and building from absolutely nothing America's first navy.

As if all that were not enough, after a trip to Paris to assist Benjamin Franklin in negotiating an alliance with France, Adams hurried home in the summer of 1779 to write the Massachusetts state constitution, a document which included many features that would be echoed in the U.S. Constitution eight years later, including strict separation of powers and a legislature composed of two separate representative bodies.

THE BOSTON TEA PARTY On Dec. 16, 1773, a group of 30 to 130 men, many of them dressed as Mohawk warriors, boarded three British ships and dumped 342 chests of tea into Boston Harbor in protest of the Tea Act, which imposed a duty on all tea sold in America by the British-owned East India Company, the only importer authorized to sell tea in the New World. The resulting conflict rapidly escalated into the Revolutionary War.

In some ways—despite his later election as president—Adams' star never shone as brightly as during those years leading up to the Revolution and America's battle for independence. He was dispatched back to Europe in late 1779, where he stayed for the remainder of the Revolutionary War until he and Franklin negotiated its end in 1783. Historians credit the combination of Franklin's tact and Adams' dogged insistence on terms favorable to America as critical to the successful conclusion of the treaty with Britain. The two men came to dislike each other, but they may have been America's most effective good cop/bad cop duo ever.

If Franklin and Adams were good cop/bad cop, then Adams and Thomas Jefferson, who arrived in France in 1784, were the original odd couple. Over the course of several months, the elegant, erudite and ever-collected Virginian forged a deep and abiding friendship with Adams and Abigail, who had joined John in France earlier that year. The relationship would be severely tested in the years ahead as the two men came to espouse diametrically opposed philosophies of government. Adams, the realist, believed a strong executive and federal government would be necessary to guard against the dangers of mob rule; Jefferson, the idealist, believed a strong central government was the greater threat to freedom and he believed, with an almost mystical fervor, in the wisdom of "the people."

Adams was sent to London in 1785 to become America's first ambassador to Great Britain—Jefferson

INTOLERABLE In 1774, the First Continental Congress was convened in Carpenter's Hall (right, with a handwritten list of attendees) in Philadelphia, then America's largest city, to address the so-called Coercive or Intolerable Acts, a series of measures intended to punish the colonists—and Massachusetts in particular—for the Boston Tea Party, and to establish the authority of the British Crown in the colonies. Among other "intolerable" acts, the provisions enabled British authorities to take over private buildings and homes to quarter soldiers, dissolve or reconfigure supposedly representative bodies as they saw fit, and even close ports like Boston to trade entirely. When Congress voted to support Massachusetts, Adams described it as "one of the happiest days of my life."

"*There is danger from all men. The only maxim of a free government ought to be to trust no man living with power to endanger the public liberty.*" JOHN ADAMS

NAVAL BEGINNING
The merchant ship *Black Prince* was acquired in 1775, renamed the USS *Alfred*, and became the first warship in the newly formed Continental Navy. In December of that year, it became the first ship to hoist the Grand Union flag—a precursor to the Stars and Stripes, which became the official American flag in 1777.

51

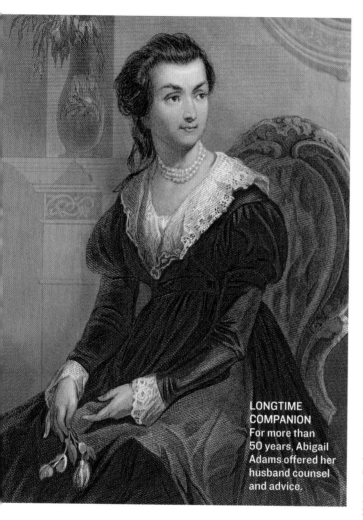

LONGTIME COMPANION
For more than 50 years, Abigail Adams offered her husband counsel and advice.

national icon and America's first president, George Washington. Adams, never one to mince words, described the vice presidency as "the most insignificant office that ever the invention of man contrived or his imagination conceived." For eight years, he dutifully supported all the administration's policies and even cast the deciding vote on Senate ties some 30 times, more than any vice president in history. But he was discouraged from speaking on the Senate floor and largely left out of important policy discussions with Washington's Cabinet members. (The executive branch viewed him as a quasi-legislative officer due to his Senate duties, and the legislative branch viewed him as a quasi-executive officer due to his allegiance to the president.) For eight years, the voluble Adams suffered, largely in silence.

His single term as president from 1797–1801 was star-crossed. He danced a fine line between the position of his own Federalist Party in support of Great Britain—Alexander Hamilton and the merchant class believed that trade with England represented the new nation's best chance at prosperity—and the pro-France leanings of Thomas Jefferson's Democratic-Republicans, who felt that the newly formed United States owed its allegiance to the French, who had supported America in its war of independence and whose revolution, while brutally violent, still represented American ideals. Adams was able to keep America out of the conflict between the two great powers, but managed to alienate supporters of both sides in the process. That outcome was undoubtedly the best for his nation, but Adams took considerable damage politically, one reason perhaps for his willingness to support the Alien and Sedition Acts, which led to blatant political prosecutions of journalists considered favorable to the Republicans. Adams later termed it the worst mistake of his presidency.

With the Federalists increasingly unpopular, Adams was defeated in his bid for a second presidential term. It was Jefferson's turn to step into the spotlight. But the nation Jefferson governed would have been quite different without the vital contributions of his friend and great rival. ★

spent time with him there, too—where he endured high-handed neglect from the British authorities during his three-year stay. While the Constitutional Convention was being held back home in Philadelphia, Adams was in London, stifled by a diplomatic role for which he was ill-suited.

POLITICAL PAIN

Of course, it would be hard to imagine a position more spectacularly wrong for the action-oriented Adams than his next job, as vice president to the

THE PRESIDENT
By the time Adams entered
the White House—he and
Abigail were the first to live
there—his Federalist Party
was in decline and he was
surrounded by enemies.

The Rules for Governing

The Virginians were among the first to arrive in Philadelphia on May 14, 1787, for the convention that forever defined the shape of American government. Over the course of the next 11 days, while they waited for representatives from the other states to appear, the Virginia delegates—including George Washington, George Mason and James Madison, who would keep copious notes of the proceedings—hashed over Madison's outline for a federal government. By the time the convention

THE PRESIDENT
George Washington (on raised platform at far right) said very little during the convention, but his mere presence insured that the proceedings would be viewed with great seriousness by the public at large.

officially began on May 25, they were ready to present their proposal. Though arguments would rage—and delegates would come and go—over the course of the next four months, that original Virginia Plan would provide many of the Constitution's most essential elements.

The first order of business was the selection of a president—the term in that case hewing to its original meaning as one who "presides"—and it was no surprise when Robert Morris of Pennsylvania rose to nominate George Washington for the job. The delegates gave their unanimous consent and Washington, resplendent in his Continental Army uniform, took his place in a high-backed chair set on a raised platform, where he could witness the goings-on below him in regal silence. The delegates were divided on several key questions. How much power should the federal government have relative to the states? How should representation in the Congress be apportioned? How would the smaller

QUIET LEADERSHIP
George Washington's main goal at the Constitutional Convention was to keep order and provide a deciding vote on a number of proposals.

states be protected from being dominated by the larger ones? How shall the president of the new nation be elected to office? And what should the delegates do about slavery? Vociferous debates ensued on all these topics as the convention stretched on into the hot summer months and beyond.

In the end, after all the haggling, the delegates agreed to several key compromises that enabled almost all of them to sign on to the new constitution. Yes, as Madison proposed on the convention's second day, there would be three branches of government, with a bicameral (two-chambered) legislature (Congress), a president leading an executive branch, and a Supreme Court the arbiter of law atop the judiciary. To protect the rights of the smaller states, one of the legislative chambers, called the Senate, would be composed of two representatives from each state, thereby assuring tiny Rhode Island the same power in that chamber as much larger New York or Pennsylvania. But in the other chamber, called the House of Representatives, representation would be based on population, ensuring that in that chamber the larger states would tend to hold sway. In that way, both large and small would be provided with protection against the other. For purposes of determining each state's population—and hence its number of seats in the House of Representatives—slaves would be counted as three-fifths of a person, less than one full person, as the Southern states had proposed in hopes of enhancing their Congressional representation, but more than nothing, as delegates from the Northern states had argued should be the case, given that plantation owners treated slaves as property, rather than human beings in need of representation. As to slavery itself, the delegates took a pass, agreeing to allow the importation of slaves for at least the next 10 years. The final document gave the federal government clear authority over the states, but also specified that any powers not delegated to the federal government would devolve to the states and, furthermore, that each state would be required to respect and honor the laws of every other state.

SUMMER SWELTER
The weather during the Philadelphia convention was described as "unbearably hot and humid."

The last issue to be settled was the system for selecting the president. The delegates' aristocratic prejudices—including fear of an "excess of democracy" and an ongoing suspicion of the less-affluent classes—doomed the notion of the president being elected by direct popular vote. So did the desire of the smaller states to retain a measure of influence in the process not based solely on their population size. In the end, Roger Sherman of Connecticut, who had come up with the winning compromise concerning representation in Congress, offered another canny proposal: The president would be selected by state electors, with the number based on the size of each state's congressional delegation, including its members in both the House and Senate. Again, this involved granting somewhat outsize influence to the smaller states, a concession that broke the impasse and enabled the convention to complete its work.

Fully 52 of the convention's 55 delegates voted for the plan. Only George Mason and Edmund Randolph of Virginia, and Elbridge Gerry of Massachusetts, voted nay out of concern that the Constitution contained no guarantee of individual rights. Finally, on Sept. 17, the convention that Madison declared would "decide forever the fate of republican government" was over. Now, the weary delegates could head home to face the daunting task of getting their remarkable document ratified.

Enacting Freedom

As a late—and much-debated— addition to the Constitution, the original 10 amendments still do much to shape the country we are today.

A MERICANS OFTEN FORGET HOW many elements of our system of government were the result of compromise and savvy political maneuvering on the part of the Founders. The Bill of Rights—the term is used to refer to the original 10 amendments to the Constitution—might not have existed at all were it not for the stubborn insistence on the part of three key delegates to the Constitutional Convention, most notably George Mason, that the Constitution alone did not sufficiently protect the individual rights of American citizens against the power of the new federal government. Fully 11 of the original 13 states already had approved bills of rights protecting individuals against overweening state power, Mason and others argued, so why shouldn't there be a national bill of rights as well?

Mason's effort to have a bill of rights included in the original draft of the Constitution was soundly rejected

THE ORIGINAL DOCUMENTS Congress commissioned 14 official copies of the Bill of Rights (one for the federal government and one for each of the original 13 states).

Congress OF THE United States

begun and held at the City of New York, on
Wednesday the Fourth of March, one thousand and seven hundred and eighty nine

THE Conventions of a number of the states, having at the time of their adopting the Constitution, expressed a desire, in order to prevent misconstruction or abuse of its powers, that further declaratory and restrictive clauses should be added: And as extending the ground of public confidence in the Government, will best ensure the beneficent ends of its institution.

RESOLVED by the Senate and House of Representatives of the United States of America, in Congress assembled, two thirds of both Houses concurring, that the following Articles be proposed to the Legislatures of the several States, as amendments to the Constitution of the United States, all, or any of which Articles, when ratified by three fourths of the said Legislatures, to be valid to all intents and purposes, as part of the said Constitution, viz.

ARTICLES in addition to, and Amendment of the Constitution of the United States of America, proposed by Congress, and ratified by the Legislatures of the several States, pursuant to the fifth Article of the original Constitution.

Article the first... After the first enumeration required by the first Article of the Constitution, there shall be one Representative for every thirty thousand, until the number shall amount to one hundred, after which the proportion shall be so regulated by Congress, that there shall be not less than one hundred Representatives, nor less than one Representative for every forty thousand persons, until the number of Representatives shall amount to two hundred, after which the proportion shall be so regulated by Congress, that there shall not be less than two hundred Representatives, nor more than one Representative for every fifty thousand persons.

Article the second... No law, varying the compensation for the services of the Senators and Representatives, shall take effect, until an election of Representatives shall have intervened.

Article the third... Congress shall make no law respecting an establishment of religion, or prohibiting the free exercise thereof; or abridging the freedom of speech, or of the press; or the right of the people peaceably to assemble, and to petition the Government for a redress of grievances.

Article the fourth... A well regulated militia, being necessary to the security of a free State, the right of the people to keep and bear Arms, shall not be infringed.

Article the fifth... No Soldier shall, in time of peace be quartered in any house, without the consent of the Owner, nor in time of war, but in a manner to be prescribed by law.

Article the sixth... The right of the people to be secure in their persons, houses, papers, and effects, against unreasonable searches and seizures, shall not be violated, and no Warrants shall issue, but upon probable cause, supported by oath or affirmation, and particularly describing the place to be searched, and the persons or things to be seized.

Article the seventh... No person shall be held to answer for a capital, or otherwise infamous crime, unless on a presentment or indictment of a Grand Jury, except in cases arising in the land or naval forces, or in the Militia, when in actual service in time of War or public danger; nor shall any person be subject for the same offence to be twice put in jeopardy of life or limb; nor shall be compelled in any criminal case to be a witness against himself, nor be deprived of life, liberty, or property, without due process of law; nor shall private property be taken for public use, without just compensation.

Article the eighth... In all criminal prosecutions, the accused shall enjoy the right to a speedy and public trial, by an impartial jury of the State and district wherein the crime shall have been committed, which district shall have been previously ascertained by law, and to be informed of the nature and cause of the accusation; to be confronted with the witnesses against him; to have compulsory process for obtaining witnesses in his favor, and to have the Assistance of Counsel for his defence.

Article the ninth... In suits at common law, where the value in controversy shall exceed twenty dollars, the right of trial by jury shall be preserved, and no fact tried by a jury, shall be otherwise re-examined in any Court of the United States, than according to the rules of the common law.

Article the tenth... Excessive bail shall not be required, nor excessive fines imposed, nor cruel and unusual punishments inflicted.

Article the eleventh... The enumeration in the Constitution, of certain rights, shall not be construed to deny or disparage others retained by the people.

Article the twelfth... The powers not delegated to the United States by the Constitution, nor prohibited by it to the States, are reserved to the States respectively, or to the people.

STILL DISSATISFIED Even after the Bill of Rights was approved, George Mason believed the Constitution did not do enough to protect individual rights.

"Let us never lose sight of this…maxim —that all power was originally lodged in, and consequently is derived from, the people."

GEORGE MASON

at the Constitutional Convention in 1787. Some historians have speculated that this failure was simply the result of fatigue—after four grueling months of intense negotiations in the steamy Philadelphia summer heat, the delegates were itching to get home to their families and their normal lives. Others suggest that some delegates worried that any enumeration of specific rights might be interpreted to mean that these were the *only* rights to be protected. But the greatest reason may have been that James Madison and the other drafters of the Constitution simply considered a bill of rights unnecessary. The first two articles of their beloved document clearly defined the powers of Congress and the presidency; in Madison's eyes, that was quite enough.

As it turned out, this peremptory rejection proved to be a political blunder as several states, including New York, Massachusetts and Virginia, declared

themselves deeply opposed to the Constitution without any guarantee of individual rights. In Virginia, Anti-Federalists—those opposed to a strong federal government—recruited James Monroe to run for Congress against Madison, an effort that might well have succeeded had Madison not pledged to shepherd a bill of rights through Congress if elected. There was dissent in other states, too. As ratification of the Constitution became increasingly probable, New York, a hotbed of Anti-Federalist sentiment, threatened to go on its own, rather than join a union without a governing bill of rights. That first Congress, elected after the Constitution was ratified in 1789, may have been dominated by Federalists, but at the state and local level, the support for a bill of rights was extremely strong.

Madison's shift in favor of the idea was likely a combination of political expediency and a desire to eliminate the possibility that those pushing for a bill of rights might call for a second constitutional convention that he feared could undo all the work he had put in to create the carefully balanced form of government the Constitution mandates. He also may have been swayed by a letter from Thomas Jefferson, away in Paris representing American interests and thus absent for the Constitutional Convention and its aftermath. Jefferson urged his friend to support a bill of rights, arguing that only a national declaration of individual rights could address the wide disparity of rights guaranteed by the states; he described a bill of rights as "what the people are entitled to against every government on Earth, general or particular, and what no government should refuse, or rest on inference."

LONG JOURNEY
James Madison introduced a series of proposed amendments—what would ultimately become the Bill of Rights—in the summer of 1789. It took more than two years for the final document to be ratified.

Even George Washington, America's indispensable leader, was in favor.

Madison's original draft presented to the House of Representatives proposed a series of 20 amendments—technically he proposed eight amendments, but his fourth eventually became the basis of 10 separate amendments and his first included three—to be inserted at relevant places within the existing Constitution. His influences were many. The right to a trial by jury came from Britain's Magna Carta; the right to bear arms and the prohibition against cruel and unusual punishment from England's own bill of rights enacted in 1689; much of the rest was based on Virginia's Declaration of Rights, largely composed by Anti-Federalist George Mason. An eight-member House select committee made a number of changes before presenting the new document to the entire House of Representatives

QUIET START For the first century after it was ratified, the Supreme Court did not apply the Bill of Rights to its rulings, maintaining that the states—and not the federal government—held the most sway over its citizens.

on July 21, 1789. Debate raged for 11 days and resulted in a number of changes, none more important than the decision, forcefully argued by Connecticut's Roger Sherman, to place the Bill of Rights at the end of the Constitution rather than inserting it within the existing text, thereby keeping the document "inviolate." The 17 resulting amendments were passed by the House and sent along to the Senate, which made a number of changes of its own, most notably eliminating the application of parts of the Bill of Rights to the states. A joint House-Senate conference hammered out the differences between the two versions and produced the 12 amendments that were sent to the states for ratification. The first two amendments dealt with the apportionment of representatives and the mode through which members of Congress could grant themselves raises. Neither received the requisite approval from three-quarters of the states, thereby making the third amendment in the draft its first, and reducing the number of amendments to 10, which were fully ratified by every state in the union by the end of 1791. While the two rejected amendments were well-intentioned, it seems inconceivable that two mundane provisions like these should precede what became the towering First Amendment as we know it today.

As inclined as we are to honor the protections the Bill of Rights provides for all of us, it is worth noting that for the first century and a half of the nation's existence, those 10 amendments had little impact on American life. It wasn't until the 20th century and the rise of new voices on the national scene that the Supreme Court began applying the Bill of Rights more widely. The due process clause of the 14th Amendment, ratified in 1868, was interpreted by the Court to extend most of the elements of the Bill of Rights (not just the original due process clause in the Sixth Amendment) to state as well as federal action through the doctrine of "incorporation"—a principle first articulated in a seminal freedom of speech case, *Gitlow v. New York*, 1925—thereby greatly expanding the scope of the Bill of Rights.

Some of the amendments have remained relatively unimportant. The Third Amendment, limiting the "quartering" of soldiers in private homes, has little or no application in modern life; the Ninth, which specifically addressed the fear that any enumeration of rights should not be "construed to deny or disparage others retained by the people," proved to be less necessary than first thought; and the 10th, which limits the power of the federal government to the role specifically defined by the Constitution and intended to mollify the Anti-Federalists who feared a federal government run rampant, while not irrelevant, has been invoked far less often than the more influential amendments.

But oh, the other seven amendments! Imagine for a moment what life might be like without them. Without the seminal First Amendment, the government could prevent us from speaking freely, from worshipping (or not) wherever we want, from protesting peacefully, and from reporting honestly what is going on in the society (freedom of the press). Without the controversial Second Amendment, the government could, if it so wished, ban all private ownership of guns. (Many would support such a ban, arguing that the language of the amendment, justifying gun ownership as necessary for a "well-regulated militia," should never have been interpreted to guarantee private ownership of guns. But the Supreme Court, most notably in *District of Columbia v. Heller*, 2008, affirmed the right to private ownership, forcing gun-control advocates to focus on particular classes of guns such as assault weapons, and other protective measures such as more extensive background checks and limitations on the size of the magazines—and hence the number of bullets—that an individual weapon can carry.)

Without the Fourth Amendment, the police could enter our homes whenever they were so inclined, search wherever they wished, and seize our personal property for any reason whatsoever. This amendment

RESPECTED LEADER Connecticut's Roger Sherman contributed to several of the nation's most important documents.

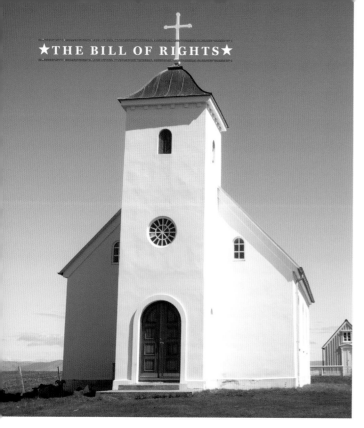

SEPARATION OF CHURCH AND STATE The first clause in the Bill of Rights firmly establishes that Congress will not interfere with freedom of religion.

is the source of the famous "probable cause" language, which has been the standard used by courts to determine the legality of a police search. Any evidence gathered without probable cause has repeatedly been ruled inadmissible in court proceedings.

The Fifth Amendment further defines our individual rights within the criminal justice system, banning the prosecution of any individual for the same offense more than once (double jeopardy), requiring an indictment by a grand jury before any person can be charged with a crime, and granting every defendant the right to refuse to testify against him or herself ("taking the Fifth," as it has come to be known). Without these critical protections, Americans would be rendered nearly helpless in the face of an all-powerful prosecution.

The Sixth Amendment is equally fundamental, and its guarantees are now taken for granted by every American. When you are arrested and charged with a crime, you have the right to be tried in a timely manner by a local jury, to know the nature of the charges against you, to call witnesses on your behalf, and to be represented by counsel at trial. Without the Sixth Amendment, none of these fundamental protections would be guaranteed. The Seventh Amendment extends the right to a trial by jury to civil as well as criminal cases, and the Eighth prohibits excessively high bail and any punishment judged "cruel and unusual." This last phrase has been much debated, particularly as it does or does not apply to capital punishment, or to particular forms of capital punishment.

There have been 17 additional amendments to the Constitution in the more than two centuries since the Bill of Rights became law. A few of these have proved as influential as the original 10. The 13th Amendment, ratified in 1865, abolished slavery for good in the United States. The 15th Amendment (1869) guaranteed people of color the right to vote; the 19th (1920) did the same for women. Perhaps the most influential of all has been the 14th Amendment (1868), which not only extended the right of due process to those charged with state offenses, but also mandated that no state shall "deny to any person within its jurisdiction the equal protection of the laws." This provision became the basis for the Supreme Court's decision in *Brown v. Board of Education* (1954), which declared school segregation inherently unequal. It also opened the floodgates for a host of challenges in the South to the system of Jim Crow, which had institutionalized segregation in every conceivable corner of public life, including restaurants, lunch counters, hotels, bars, hospitals, and even bathrooms.

But those first 10 amendments remain the bedrock of our individual freedoms. And for those, we owe much to the tiny man from Virginia, James Madison, whose well-honed political instincts enabled him to overcome his social awkwardness and shepherd the eventual Bill of Rights through a fractious Congress and on to ratification. His presidency may have been flawed, but his vital contributions to the Constitution and the Bill of Rights will forever earn him a place in the American pantheon. ★

What It Says

FREE SPEECH
Americans have a right to gather and protest peacefully.

FIRST AMENDMENT

Congress shall make no law respecting an establishment of religion, or prohibiting the free exercise thereof; or abridging the freedom of speech, or of the press; or the right of the people peaceably to assemble, and to petition the Government for a redress of grievances.

SECOND AMENDMENT

A well regulated Militia, being necessary to the security of a free State, the right of the people to keep and bear Arms, shall not be infringed.

THIRD AMENDMENT

No Soldier shall, in time of peace be quartered in any house, without the consent of the Owner, nor in time of war, but in a manner to be prescribed by law.

FOURTH AMENDMENT

The right of the people to be secure in their persons, houses, papers, and effects, against unreasonable searches and seizures, shall not be violated, and no Warrants shall issue, but upon probable cause, supported by Oath or affirmation, and particularly describing the place to be searched, and the persons or things to be seized.

FIFTH AMENDMENT

No person shall be held to answer for a capital, or otherwise infamous crime, unless on a presentment or indictment of a Grand Jury, except in cases arising in the land or naval forces, or in the Militia, when in actual service in time of War or public danger; nor shall any person be subject for the same offence to be twice put in jeopardy of life or limb; nor shall be compelled in any criminal case to be a witness against himself, nor be deprived of life, liberty, or property, without due process of law; nor shall private property be taken for public use, without just compensation.

SIXTH AMENDMENT

In all criminal prosecutions, the accused shall enjoy the right to a speedy and public trial, by an impartial jury of the State and district wherein the crime shall have been committed, which district shall have been previously ascertained by law, and to be informed of the nature and cause of the accusation; to be confronted with the witnesses against him; to have compulsory process for obtaining witnesses in his favor, and to have the Assistance of Counsel for his defence.

SEVENTH AMENDMENT

In Suits at common law, where the value in controversy shall exceed twenty dollars, the right of trial by jury shall be preserved, and no fact tried by a jury, shall be otherwise re-examined in any Court of the United States, than according to the rules of the common law.

EIGHTH AMENDMENT

Excessive bail shall not be required, nor excessive fines imposed, nor cruel and unusual punishments inflicted.

NINTH AMENDMENT

The enumeration in the Constitution, of certain rights, shall not be construed to deny or disparage others retained by the people.

10TH AMENDMENT

The powers not delegated to the United States by the Constitution, nor prohibited by it to the States, are reserved to the States respectively, or to the people.

THOMAS JEFFERSON

Man of the People

For Jefferson, one word defined the most critical goal of the American Revolution: freedom.

THOMAS JEFFERSON WAS A MAN OF MANY contradictions. Preternaturally shy and deeply averse to public speaking, he nonetheless mastered the art of politics and rose to the highest office in the land. An author of the nation's founding declaration of human rights, he nonetheless owned slaves and came to accept slavery as an institution that could not practically be abolished. An admitted racist who wrote openly of what he viewed as the inferiority of African Americans, he—the evidence strongly suggests—fathered at least one child, and perhaps several children, with one of the women he enslaved, Sally Hemings. A fervent opponent to the establishment of a strong central government, he nonetheless used his executive authority to approve the Louisiana Purchase, a sweeping federal acquisition that effectively doubled the size of the nation. In all these ways, Jefferson remains a distinctly American enigma, whose character and essence is likely to be debated for as long as the American republic exists.

He was born in 1743 in Albemarle County, in the foothills of the Blue Ridge Mountains of Virginia, to Peter Jefferson, a prosperous surveyor and farmer who owned 60 slaves, and Jane Randolph Jefferson, who descended from one of the region's most prominent families. (He wrote almost nothing about his mother throughout his life, leading many historians to conclude that his relationship with her was a difficult one.) His father died when Jefferson was 14, and rather than stay at home with his mother—further evidence of a less-than-ideal connection—Jefferson chose to board with his local schoolmaster and tutor. He attended the

BOOKWORM Jefferson was a voracious reader and had many of his books, like those above, bound in leather. When the British destroyed much of the Library of Congress in 1814, Jefferson replenished it from his own personal collection of books, which numbered in the thousands.

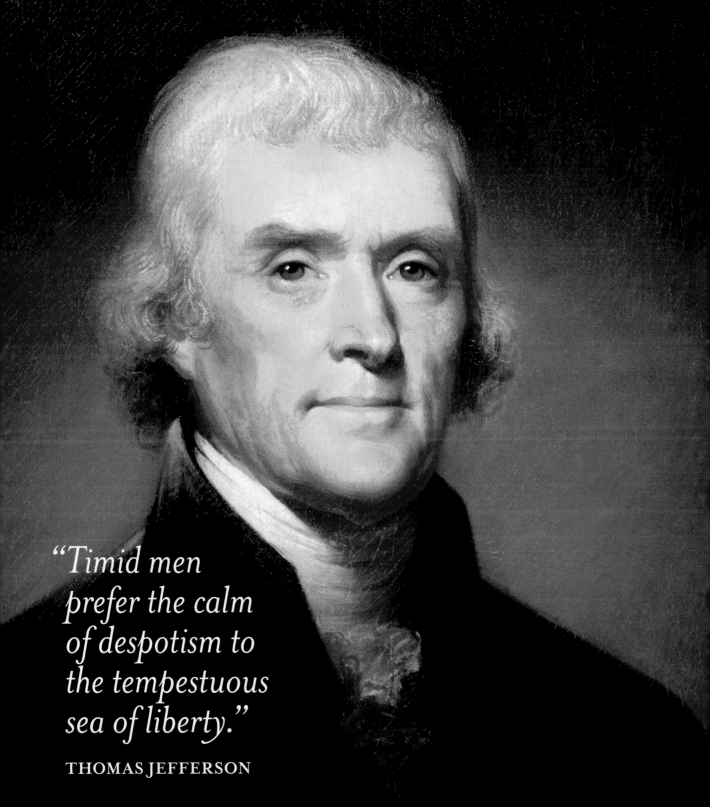

"Timid men prefer the calm of despotism to the tempestuous sea of liberty."

THOMAS JEFFERSON

elegant College of William and Mary in Williamsburg, where he established himself as a tireless pupil, reputedly spending 15 hours a day reading and studying, for the most part under the tutelage of a pair of scholars—George Wythe and William Small—who schooled him on moral philosophy, the law, mathematics and science. (He had already mastered both Latin and Greek before his arrival at college.) While James Madison and John Adams were certainly learned, and Benjamin Franklin may have been a genuine genius, it seems fair to judge Jefferson as the best-educated.

JOINING THE FIGHT

Jefferson's early adulthood was taken up with his dual responsibilities as a lawyer and young farmer. His shyness prevented him from performing well in

"Every government degenerates when trusted to the rulers of the people alone. The people themselves are the only safe depositories."
THOMAS JEFFERSON

BELOVED RETREAT Jefferson designed and directed the construction of his cherished home—an initial drawing is shown above—after inheriting some 5,000 acres of land from his father when he was 26. He named the elegant neoclassical structure Monticello (Italian for "little hill") and built it on the summit of an 850-foot peak in the Southwest Mountains. Jefferson is buried on the grounds in the area now known as the Monticello Cemetery.

A

SUMMARY VIEW

OF THE

RIGHTS

OF

BRITISH AMERICA.

SET FORTH IN SOME

RESOLUTIONS

INTENDED FOR THE

INSPECTION

OF THE PRESENT

DELEGATES

OF THE

PEOPLE OF VIRGINIA.

NOW IN

CONVENTION.

BY A NATIVE, AND MEMBER OF THE
HOUSE OF BURGESSES.

WILLIAMSBURG:
PRINTED BY CLEMENTINA RIND

the courtroom, but his written briefs and opinions established him as a formidable legal scholar. Among his many passions were his interest in architecture and his love of neoclassical design, first seen in Monticello, his beloved home—construction began in

CALLING OUT A KING In his *A Summary View of the Rights of British America* (left), Jefferson addressed himself directly to King George III, noting that "kings are the servants, not the proprietors of the people. Open your breast, sire, to liberal and expanded thought. Let not the name of George the third be a blot in the page of history." On July 9, 1776, after Britain turned a deaf ear to American demands, colonists pulled down a statue of George (above) from its pedestal in New York City.

1768 and never really ended—on the top of a mountain near Charlottesville, Virginia. As Monticello was taking shape, Jefferson took another important step: He won election to the Virginia House of Burgesses, positioning himself in politics at a critical juncture, when the two most actively rebellious colonies—Massachusetts and Virginia—were beginning to frame the argument for independence.

In 1772, he married Martha Wayles Skelton—a relationship which seems to have been one of genuine love and devotion. Martha gave birth to six children with Jefferson, though only two daughters lived to adulthood. Martha herself, who may have been diabetic and was in ill health throughout the marriage,

71

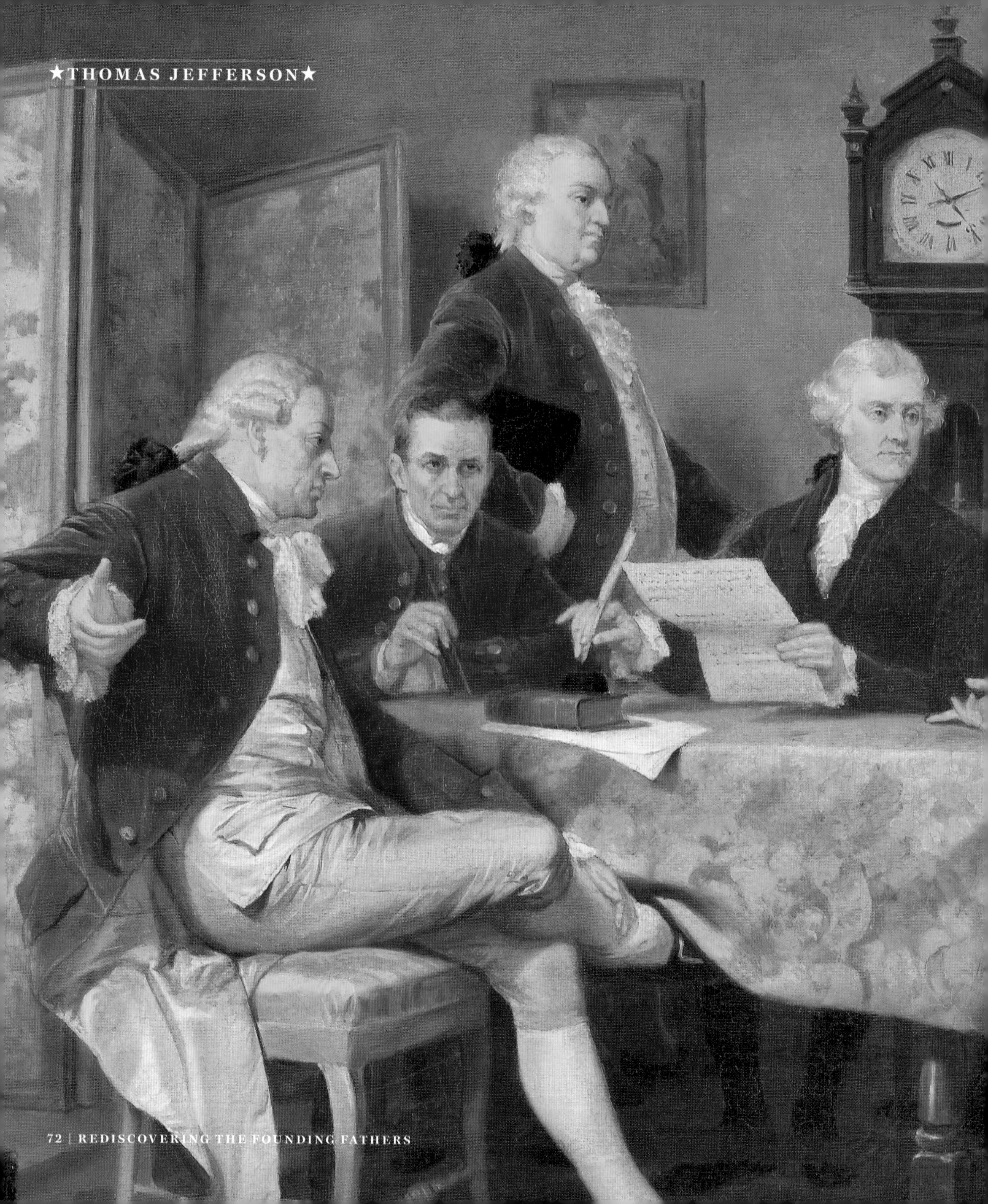

WRITING HISTORY In the 19th century,
Alonzo Chappel painted this fanciful version of
the five members of the drafting committee for the
Declaration of Independence. From left: Robert
Livingston, Roger Sherman, John Adams (standing),
Thomas Jefferson and Benjamin Franklin. In fact,
Livingston and Sherman had very little to do with the
document. Jefferson's rough draft is shown above.

"I never considered a difference of opinion in politics, in religion, in philosophy, as cause for withdrawing from a friend."

THOMAS JEFFERSON

died in 1782, plunging her husband into what friends described as inconsolable grief.

Jefferson's devotion to the cause of independence only grew more passionate as the years went by and the British outrages continued. In 1774, he authored *A Summary View of the Rights of British America*; its bold assertion of America's right to withdraw its loyalty from the British monarchy established Jefferson as an eloquent voice for freedom in Virginia and beyond. It also made him a logical choice as a delegate to the Second Continental Congress, where John Adams immediately saw the elegant but gangly young Virginian—Jefferson was 6-foot-2, a truly imposing height for the era—as an important ally in his effort to urge his fellow colonists toward independence. When both men were named to the committee to draft a declaration of the American position, Adams urged his fellow members to let Jefferson, a gifted and eloquent writer, take on the task. The result was a document (see page 32) whose opening paragraphs remain today among the nation's most cherished. In the centuries to come, as a changing country expanded the meaning of the phrase "all men are created equal" to include women and people of color and of differing sexual orientations, it became a rallying cry for civil rights at home and abroad. "I have a dream," Martin Luther King Jr. declared in his incomparable speech from the steps of the Lincoln Memorial in 1963, "that one day this nation will rise up, live out the true meaning of its creed—'We hold these truths to be self-evident, that all men are created equal.'"

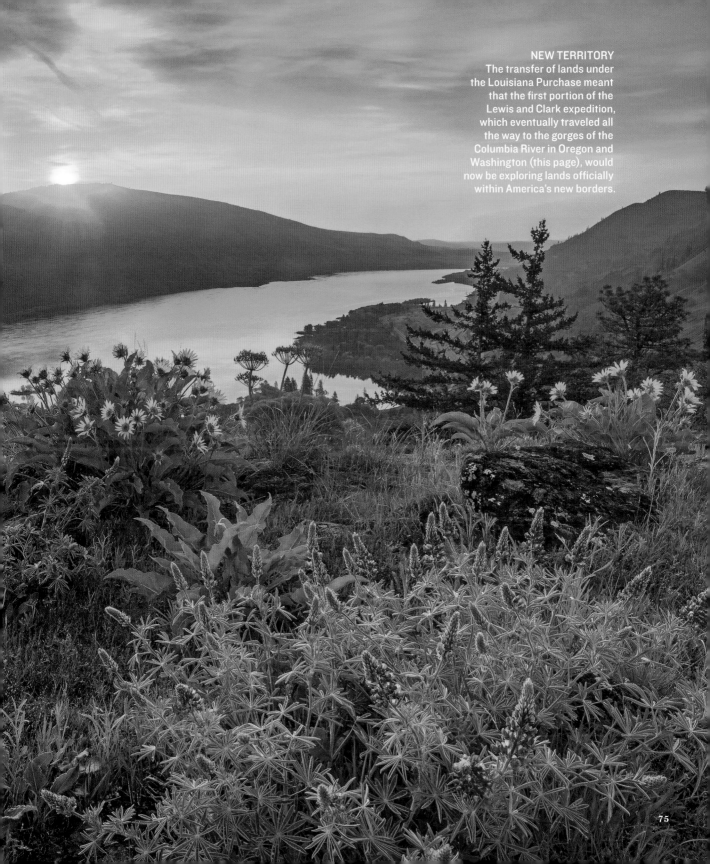

HOLDING OFFICE
Jefferson was the first president to be inaugurated in Washington, D.C. He won reelection by capturing more than 70% of the popular vote and an electoral count of 162 to 14.

THOMAS JEFFERSON
1743–1826

EUROPE AND BACK

Jefferson's star dimmed a bit during the decade or so after the Declaration; he played no role in the military triumph of his fellow Virginian, George Washington, and he was in Paris as his new nation's representative when the U.S. Constitution was being shaped, in large measure through the brilliance of another Virginian, James Madison. (Jefferson and Madison, who would become staunch allies and friends, exchanged letters during the Constitutional Convention and many of the ideas that made their way into the final document reflected principles Jefferson had enunciated in Virginia—most notably the strict separation of church and state—but he had little direct influence on the outcome.)

The nation had not forgotten him, however, and when he returned from his largely fruitless five years in Paris—he did find time to pursue what was apparently a torrid relationship with a beautiful but married Anglo-Italian woman named Maria Cosway—he was appointed by President George Washington as America's first secretary of state in 1789. During Jefferson's years in the Washington administration, the fundamental conflict that would define his remaining years in politics and lead to the creation of the nation's first political parties was intensifying. On one side were Jefferson and his ally James Madison, opponents of a strong central government and firm believers in the virtues of an agrarian America. On the other were John Adams, Alexander Hamilton and, to a lesser degree, George Washington, all of whom viewed a strong federal government as the only means to bind the colonies into a single cohesive nation, capable of resisting the danger of mob rule while ensuring peace and tranquility for all its citizens regardless of region or class. Hamilton in particular also viewed the nation's merchant class and the rise of cities as the likely source of the nation's future prosperity and hence where the federal government's efforts should be directed, rather than to the agrarian class—the rich planters and plantation owners in particular—whom Jefferson saw as the backbone of the nation.

TRAGIC LIFE Martha Jefferson gave birth to seven children but only two daughters would live to adulthood, and Martha herself was frequently ill. Historians speculate that she never fully recovered from the birth of her last child, Lucy Elizabeth, dying four months later.

PARTY POLITICS

Jefferson's discomfort with the Federalist slant of Washington's policies and what he saw as insufficient concern for individual rights—he was a strong proponent of a bill of rights—led to the formation of America's first real political party, originally called the Republican, later the Democratic-Republican, Party. These were uncharted waters, as the very notion of an opposition "party" was novel and, to some, downright treasonous. But Jefferson felt impelled to oppose the direction in which Washington, and later Adams, was leading the country, viewing Hamilton's notion of a strong federal government—those in power quite

ACADEMIC MODEL

Jefferson's design for the University of Virginia—the view at right is looking south from the Jefferson Rotunda to Cabell Hall—called for faculty and students to be housed around a central lawn, with arcades of student rooms stretching between the professors' homes. The arrangement was intended to provoke discussion among all members of the college community representing a variety of academic disciplines.

The happy Effects of that Grand System of shutting Ports against the English !!

naturally called themselves the Federalist Party—anti-thetical to the principles of the revolution and little better than the sort of tyranny imposed on America by King George III. It was a rift that Adams and Jefferson, though they reconciled later in life, could never bridge.

Certainly Jefferson's stint as vice president under Adams from 1797–1801 did little to heal the division. (Prior to 1804, the top electoral vote-getter was named president and the candidate with the next highest total became vice president, meaning it was possible that one's main opponent in the election would end up as vice president. The 12th Amendment directed electors to cast separate votes for each of the two offices and candidates began running together as part of a single "ticket.") Given the limited power of the vice president and Jefferson's clearly stated opposition to

DISCORD AT HOME Angered by British impressment of American sailors as well as French interference in U.S. shipping, Jefferson called for the Embargo Act of 1807, which created an embargo on all foreign goods. The measure backfired, strongly damaging the U.S. economy. Political cartoons (above and right) marked public opposition to the embargo.

the Federalist agenda, it is no surprise that he wielded little influence in the Adams administration and was determined to defeat Adams in 1800 and become president himself. The election was so dirty that it is astonishing that Adams and Jefferson ever spoke to one another again: Jefferson even paid several journalists to libel Adams and damage his chances for reelection. In the end, Adams' principled position of neutrality in the ongoing conflict between Britain and France angered both Federalists, who favored the British, and Democratic-Republicans, who favored the French, and Jefferson and his running mate Aaron Burr won the election handily. Electors supporting Jefferson were told to vote for both men, but one elector was supposed to withhold his vote from Burr, thereby guaranteeing Jefferson would have the greater number of votes to be president. Alas, the plan was not properly communicated and the Democratic-Republicans delivered identical totals to both men, throwing the election into the House of Representatives, where it took 36 ballots—and considerable arm-twisting by Hamilton, who detested Burr and considered Jefferson the lesser of two evils—to get Jefferson elected.

PRESIDENT JEFFERSON

Once in office, Jefferson set about reducing the size and scope of government as he promised he would, and the public seemed to approve, though some of Jefferson's popularity was likely the result of the booming American economy, now able to openly trade with newly peaceful Britain and France. The two signature acts of Jefferson's first term also enhanced his public standing. First, the Lewis and Clark expedition to explore the American continent to its West Coast was a bold

"It is the great parent of science & of virtue; and that a nation will be great in both, always in proportion as it is free."

THOMAS JEFFERSON

statement of his belief that America's future lay in the West, a vision that nicely coincided with his preference for a more rural nation. And the Louisiana Purchase in 1803 was one of the greatest land deals in history, in which Jefferson purchased enough territory from France—Napoleon was desperate for cash—to double the size of the U.S. for the bargain price of $15 million. It was hardly the act of a man who believed in limited government, but his near-evangelical belief in the nation's need to expand overrode any reservations. These two acts, along with a growing economy, guaranteed an overwhelming victory for Jefferson in his bid for reelection in 1804. Alas, his second term was much less successful, as Britain and France resumed hostilities and Jefferson's decision to impose an embargo on goods from both nations in an attempt to produce a settlement proved disastrous to the American economy. Battered by criticism and exhausted by political warfare, he was happy to retire to private life in 1809.

His later years in Monticello were largely happy. He rose early and spent much of the day writing letters. His interest in architecture and education found confluence in the construction of the University of Virginia in Charlottesville, designed largely by Jefferson, and an elegant neoclassical memorial to his exceptional talents. He never remarried but remained extremely close with his daughter, Martha, known to most as Patsy, whom Jefferson described as "the cherished companion of his youth and the nurse of his old age." He died, deeply in debt, on July 4, 1826, on the 50th anniversary of his immortal declaration of human rights in 1776. ★

SLAVERY

America's Original Sin

INHUMAN TREATMENT
Slaves were still traded and sold right up to the eve of the Civil War, as illustrated in this slave auction, which was held in 1861 in Virginia.

Like a threatening storm cloud lurking on the horizon, the practice of slavery loomed large over the American experiment from the very beginning. The census of 1790 counted 700,000 slaves—fully 18% of the American population—and the percentages in the South were considerably higher: 43% in South Carolina, 39% in Virginia (with 300,000 slaves, the most of any state), 32% in Maryland and 26% in North Carolina. The abolitionist movement did not gather steam until the 1830s, but there were always Americans adamantly opposed to slavery and deeply disgusted by its obvious betrayal of the fundamental values on which the nation was founded. John Jay wrote in 1786: "It is much to be wished that slavery may be abolished. The honour of the States, as well as justice and humanity, in my opinion, loudly call upon them to emancipate these unhappy people. To contend for our own liberty, and to deny that blessing to others, involves an inconsistency not to be excused."

But as the state delegates gathered in Philadelphia for the Constitutional Convention in 1787, it was clear that the nation was irredeemably split on the issue, with representatives in the South unlikely to support any document that condemned slavery, which they had come to see as the very backbone of their economy. In their view there was simply no way to grow and harvest cotton, rice and tobacco without the use of slaves. (While slaves were not inexpensive, they were far cheaper than paying for labor and they could be worked relentlessly all day and punished brutally if they were not as productive as the owners wished, behavior that would never be tolerated by wage

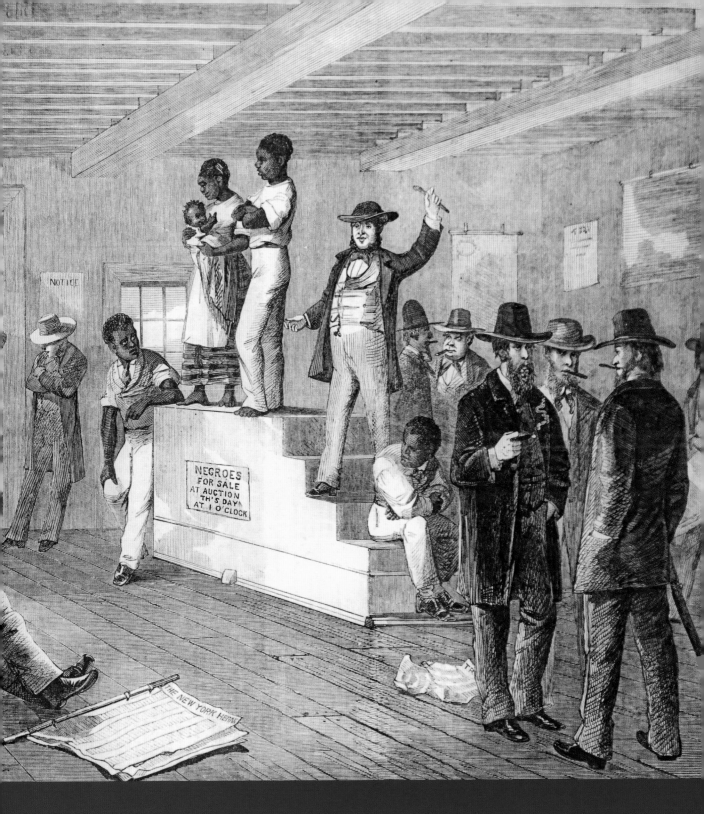

workers endowed with freedom and at least minimal protections against mistreatment.)

The framers simply ignored the issue when possible and compromised in the three instances when the subject could not be avoided. The Fugitive Slave Clause, much desired by Southern elements, forbade slaves from fleeing to nonslave states, requiring such slaves to be returned to their original locations when requested. Another clause banned Congress from prohibiting the slave trade until 1808, guaranteeing its continuance for at least 20 years after the writing of the Constitution. Finally, in an act of breathtaking gall, the delegates allowed the Southern states to count each slave as equivalent to three-fifths of a free person for the determination of their population and the number of congressional seats to which they would be entitled. The Northern faction had not wanted slaves counted at all, arguing that Southern slave owners clearly treated them as property, while Southerners who hoped to maximize their representation in Congress wanted slaves counted as full people. The absurdity of treating a man as chattel while simultaneously using his existence to enhance your own power over his freedom was impossible to

CRUEL BEGINNINGS Many of the Africans imported for slavery were forced to endure passage to America crammed into ships in the manner shown below. Later, they might be housed in dwellings like the ones at left, built for slaves on Boone Hall Plantation in Charleston, South Carolina.

"I wish from my soul that the Legislature of the State could see the policy of a gradual Abolition of Slavery..."

GEORGE WASHINGTON

miss. In the end James Madison fashioned the three-fifths compromise that enabled the Constitution to be widely accepted in both North and South.

Several Founding Fathers owned slaves at one time or another—John Adams and Alexander Hamilton were the only exceptions, and there is some debate about Hamilton—though Ben Franklin was a staunch abolitionist by 1781, and George Washington directed that the slaves under his control be freed after his death. All of them—even Jefferson and Madison—recognized the inhumanity of the practice and how toxic it would be for the American body politic. Could an American union have been formed without slavery being tolerated? There's no way to know for sure, but evidence suggests not, allowing that the very crucible of American liberty was forged in racism from the beginning. And though it would take another 75 years or so, that fundamental flaw in the American character would tear the nation apart.

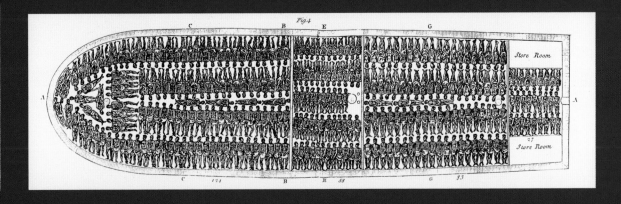

"Those who would give up essential Liberty, to purchase a little temporary Safety, deserve neither Liberty nor Safety."

BENJAMIN FRANKLIN

BENJAMIN FRANKLIN

The Genius

Almost entirely self-taught, Franklin displayed his creativity in a dizzying array of roles.

ALTHOUGH BENJAMIN FRANKLIN CAME TO THE cause of revolution later than his fellow Founding Fathers, he was in many ways the most quintessentially American of all. Where else but in America could a man reinvent himself so frequently and take on such an astonishing array of roles? Inventor, printer, scientist, diplomat, writer, philosopher, businessman, public official, urban planner, swimmer, lothario—Franklin at various points in his life was all of these, and so much more. Walt Whitman, in his poem, "Song of Myself," famously declared: "I contain multitudes." No one contained a larger horde than Franklin.

He was born in 1706, the youngest son among 17 children of a Boston soap and candlemaker, one of the less-lucrative artisan trades of the period. Money was scarce and Franklin had very little formal education as a child, and none whatsoever after the age of 10, when he went to work assisting his father. But Franklin was one of history's most brilliant autodidacts—"I do not remember when I could not read," he noted in his wildly popular, posthumously published *The Autobiography of Benjamin Franklin*—and his voracious quest for learning never ceased. As diligent as he was in his work for his father, the clever boy was clearly not destined to be a candlemaker.

His first profession, and the one that provided him with the fortune to pursue his other interests, was that of a printer. At age 12, he was apprenticed to his older brother James and spent the next four years learning his trade. He also began making his mark as a writer of exceptional skill and wit in the *New-England Courant*, the

PRACTICAL BRILLIANCE
Among Franklin's many inventions were bifocal glasses, like the pair above, with spectacles split into two parts, each with a different focal length. Franklin introduced the first pair in 1784.

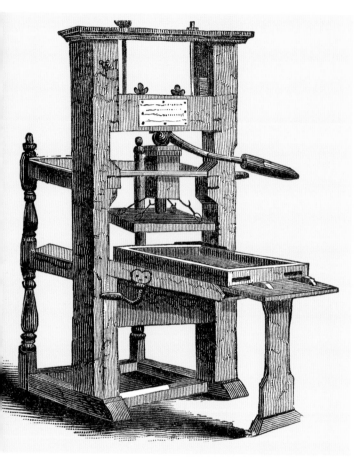

LEARNING HIS TRADE Soon after his arrival in Philadelphia, Franklin left for a brief sojourn in London, where he honed his skills on a press like the one above left, before returning to Philadelphia and starting his own printing business on Market Street (right). Among the many works he published was Thomas Dilworth's *A New Guide to the English Tongue* (above).

weekly newspaper James had established in 1721, publishing a series of 14 satirical essays—funeral orations and the pretensions of Harvard students were two of his targets—written in the voice of a middle-aged widow named Mrs. Silence Dogood. But the ambitious Franklin was not destined to be someone else's employee, either, and at the age of 16, he sneaked out of Boston and headed to New York City. Failing to find work there, he made his way to Philadelphia, the city where he rose from obscurity to become his nation's most famous citizen. For 25 years, he built his printing business—he started with a partner in 1728 but bought him out in 1730—and eventually landed a lucrative contract to produce the paper currency

for Pennsylvania, and then for New Jersey, Delaware and Maryland. By the late 1740s, he was one of the wealthiest men in the Northern colonies. Throughout this period, he continued to educate himself—he eventually mastered four languages—and to write, write, write, soon establishing himself as one of the colonies' most gifted thinkers, with a wide-ranging mind that encompassed philosophy, science and the oddities of everyday life. Many of his maxims became famous, not only his paeans to industry, such as "Early to bed and early to rise, makes a man healthy, wealthy and

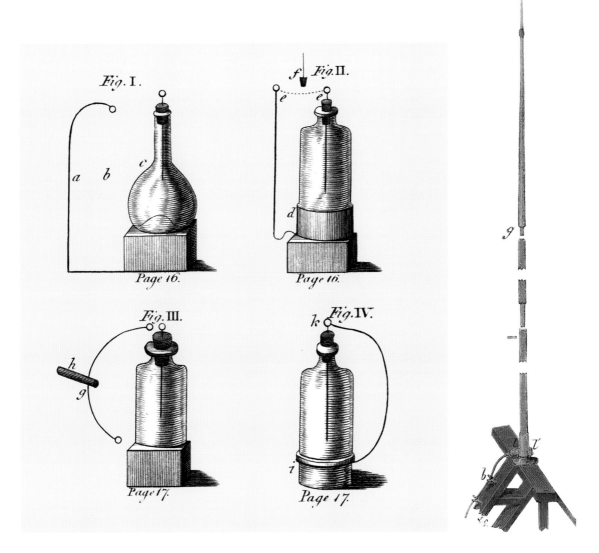

wise," but also those focused on the human condition, such as "Keep your eyes wide open before marriage, half shut afterward."

SCIENTIST AND HUSBAND

In the 1740s, Franklin began his explorations in the nascent field of electricity, including his iconic experiment in which he flew a kite during a thunderstorm to determine "whether the clouds that contain that lightning are electrified." (They were.) His advances were truly groundbreaking—they were the basis for the

ELECTRICITY EXPLORED Franklin's advances in the study of electricity were numerous, many of them resulting from his experiments with Leyden jars (above left), devices pioneered in Europe that provided the first means of storing an electric charge, which could then be manipulated by scientists to discover its properties. In 1752, Franklin invented the lightning rod (above right), which he installed on homes like those on the opposite page.

critical principle known as the law of conservation of charge—and when his findings were published in Britain and France, they made him an overnight celebrity.

PRINT PIONEER

The Newsman

In 1729, Franklin and his partner Hugh Meredith purchased the awkwardly named *The Universal Instructor in all Arts and Sciences: and Pennsylvania Gazette.* They shortened the title to the *Pennsylvania Gazette*, changed its frequency to twice a week, and eventually made it the most successful newspaper in the colonies. Like most of the early papers, it included a mix of local advertising, classified ads, help-wanted notices and a smattering of genuine news from home and abroad. It also included essays and letters to the editor, most of them written by Franklin himself under a host of pseudonyms, as well as reports on his scientific experiments. In 1754, the *Gazette* published America's first political cartoon, titled Join, or

JOIN, or DIE.

Die (above), which depicted the American colonies as segments of a snake that needed to stay together or perish. The cartoon was originally intended to urge a tight alliance between the unified colonies and Great Britain against a common opponent in the French and Indian War, but in little more than a decade it became a symbol of American determination to stay united in opposition to British oppression.

However, the *Gazette* was not the first paper in the colonies. The *New-England Courant*, a weekly publication created by Franklin's brother James, was distributed in 1721 and is considered one of the first newspapers in Boston. Andrew Bradford, who published his *American Weekly Mercury* in 1719, is credited with the first newspaper in Philadelphia. Samuel Keimer began publishing *The Universal Instructor* in 1728, just a year before Franklin bought it. All had limited readerships and editorial oddities—Keimer's paper, for example, included a page from either an encyclopedia or a dictionary with each issue. What none of the other papers had was Franklin's distinctive voice, and that ultimately made all the difference.

The Europeans were particularly impressed that these discoveries came from America, which they imagined as a place of unimaginable coarseness. Only a genuine genius could be successful in such benighted climes.

Franklin's originality of mind generated startling scientific insights, but he pursued a path that was at least as unconventional in his personal life. He took Deborah Read as his wife in 1730—their union was considered a common-law marriage, because her former husband had deserted her and she had never been formally divorced. Soon after uniting with Deborah, Franklin presented her with his infant son William, who had been born to an unidentified woman before his marriage. Deborah agreed to raise the boy as her own, though her relationship with William was always strained. Together, the couple had a son Francis, who

J. J. Crown

THE
GENERAL MAGAZINE,
AND
Historical Chronicle,
For all the *British* Plantations in *America.*
[To be Continued Monthly.]

JANUARY, 1741.

ICH DIEN

VOL. I.

PHILADELPHIA:
Printed and Sold by B. FRANKLIN.

died at age 4, and a daughter Sarah, who survived both her parents. Without tangible evidence, it is hard to determine the true nature of Benjamin and Deborah's relationship, but it is safe to say that Franklin was hardly a model husband. He was famously promiscuous and spent most of the marriage away from Deborah, in London or Paris, where he could freely indulge in what his peers termed his "dissolute" lifestyle. When Deborah died in 1774, Franklin had not seen her in 10 years.

LEADING CITIZEN

By 1748, Franklin had amassed enough wealth to essentially retire and pursue his interests without any need to concern himself with commerce. (He remained a silent partner in a printing firm that bore his name and provided him with a healthy annual income.) Over the next decade, he dedicated himself to a host of civic causes in his adopted city of Philadelphia. It

OUTSPOKEN According to popular legend, Franklin, while editor of the *Pennsylvania Gazette*, invited advertisers who complained about his paper's controversial content to a meal (above). Instead of the sumptuous feast the guests were expecting and as a means to express his disdain for their opinions, Franklin served them "sawdust pudding," a sort of cornmeal mush generally consumed by those too poor to afford anything better. During his extended time in London, Franklin lived in the house at right, the only one of his homes still standing.

was largely through Franklin's efforts that the city had a sanitation system, a volunteer fire department and the beginnings of a police force. He also pioneered the development of a library and the establishment of the College of Philadelphia, which eventually evolved into the University of Pennsylvania.

In 1757, Franklin moved to London, in part to convince the British authorities to rescind the charter that established the Penn family as the proprietors

of the Pennsylvania colony and make it a royal province. Franklin failed in this effort, but he reveled in his life as the toast of London and decided to stay. With the single exception of a two-year period in the 1760s, Franklin remained in London until 1775, hobnobbing with fellow luminaries like philosopher David Hume, explorer Captain James Cook and noted intellectual and writer Joseph Priestley. Franklin admired the British and remained hopeful that differences between the mother country and its colonies could be settled in a manner that enabled the American colonists to remain British subjects. Between 1765 and 1775, he wrote 126 newspaper stories, the bulk of which attempted to bridge the gap between the two sides. Many Americans became suspicious of Franklin's motives; some even suspected him of being a British spy. A four-hour denunciation of the Stamp Act in the British Parliament in 1766 salvaged his image at home, as Franklin began to view his British hosts less favorably. Still, he hoped for reconciliation.

The final blow for Franklin came after his ill-considered decision to send a series of letters back to America that were written by Thomas Hutchinson, the British governor of Massachusetts, in which Hutchinson recommended restricting the rights of the colonists in the wake of American protests against the Stamp Act. (Franklin had intended the letters to be read only by key decision-makers, but Samuel Adams managed to leak their essence without leaking the letters themselves.) Franklin hoped to persuade the colonists that the real problem was not the British, but rather the British representatives in America who misrepresented the colonists' situation to their masters; he hoped to persuade the British that they needed to appoint less-deceitful individuals to administer the colonies. The attempt failed miserably on both counts. The Americans were incensed by the letters and became even more militant in their resistance to British rule, while the British, angry over Franklin's release of confidential information, forced Franklin to stand silently by as he was publicly excoriated by the British solicitor general before a raucous and derisive audience of British officials. By the time he returned to America in 1775, Franklin had become convinced that independence was the only way forward.

CELEBRITY IN FRANCE

His visit home was short-lived, though he did remain long enough to assist Thomas Jefferson and John Adams in the writing of the Declaration of Independence. But then he was off to Europe again, this time to France to enlist the support of the French in America's ongoing fight for nationhood.

The decision of the Continental Congress to send Franklin as its lead representative was exceedingly wise. Franklin was a celebrity of unparalleled magnitude in France, which was gripped by a frenzied fascination with all things American. "He was not given the title of Monsieur," noted one Frenchman, "he was addressed simply as Doctor Franklin, as one would have addressed Plato or Socrates." His likeness was emblazoned everywhere, on snuffboxes, candy boxes, statues and prints; one medallion declared in Latin that Franklin "snatched the lightning from heaven and the scepter from tyrants." Some French women even had their hair styled to imitate the American's distinctive 'do. Franklin, of course, basked in the adulation and played the role of the genius frontiersman to the hilt, wearing a fur cap and a plain brown-and-white linen suit everywhere, even in the court of Versailles, where such informality would normally be considered

REVOLUTION The Pennsylvania Assembly voted unanimously in favor of selecting Franklin as a delegate to the Continental Congress, where he assisted Thomas Jefferson and John Adams in drafting the Declaration of Independence. The Congress' approval of the document was announced outside Philadelphia's Independence Hall on July 4, 1776.

THE REBELS C
THE GRE

'76.

July 4 1776

OR, THE FIRST ANNOUNCEMENT OF
DECLARATION.

"God grant that not only the love of liberty but a thorough knowledge of the rights of man may pervade all the nations of the Earth, so that a philosopher may set his foot anywhere on its surface and say: 'This is my country.'"

BENJAMIN FRANKLIN

TOAST OF THE TOWN
Franklin was embraced by French society, charming all he met, including the swells at the court of Versailles in 1778.

SLY FOX
Though it was hardly
his typical garb in
America, Franklin was
more than willing to
don a fur hat (right)
in France to reinforce
his image overseas as
a rustic genius. The
Treaty of Alliance,
which led to the entry
of France into the
Revolutionary War
on the side of the
Americans, was signed
in 1778 at the Hotel
de Coislin (opposite
page) in Paris.

BENJAMIN FRANKLIN.

Né à Boston, dans la nouvelle Angleterre le 17 Janvier 1706

Dessiné par C. N. Cochin Chevalier de l'Ordre du Roi, en 1777 et Gravé par Aug. de St. Aubin Graveur de la Bibliothèque du Roi.
Se vend à Paris chez C. N. Cochin aux Galleries du Louvre, et chez Aug de St. Aubin, rue des Mathurins.

C. N. Cochin Junr.

an affront. French society, including the aristocrats, was utterly charmed, even winking at Franklin's open pursuit of several comely French women. At 70, Franklin was beset with painful gout and kidney stones, but his libido was apparently fully functional.

In the end, Franklin succeeded sensationally. France not only recognized the fledgling United States, it also lent the Americans money and eventually sent desperately needed troops, gunpowder and ships. Without this aid, it is unlikely that even George Washington could have been victorious.

Franklin remained in Europe long enough to assist John Adams and John Jay in negotiating the peace treaty that ended the war in 1783. And he was present at the Constitutional Convention in 1787, as one of the 39 men—and the oldest, at 81—to sign the document. "I consent, sir, to this constitution," he said, "because I expect no better, and because I am not sure that it is not the best." It was classic Franklin, reflecting his natural hatred of discord and his inclination toward compromise. He died three years later, but the nation to which he helped give birth would survive. ★

Choosing the President

The Founders' system of voting values state ballots over national totals, an arrangement that has often provoked controversy.

T HE DELEGATES TO THE CONSTITU-tional Convention dealt with a number of thorny issues, none more so than the issue of how the president should be selected. Some, including constitutional architect James Madison, were in favor of allowing a popular vote to choose the chief executive, at least in theory. But Madison and his allies knew that this seemingly logical solution was certain to be opposed by the less-populous Southern states, which had forced the infamous three-fifths compromise on the convention, a Faustian bargain that allowed them to count each of their Black slaves as equivalent to three-fifths of a white citizen for the purposes of determining the

ELECTING NUMBER 29
Warren Harding dominated both the popular vote and the Electoral College in his 1920 presidential victory over Democrat James M. Cox, as the votes are presented to Congress.

A SHAMEFUL HISTORY
In 1876, Democrat Samuel Tilden won the popular vote by more than 260,000 but failed to capture enough electoral votes with three states in dispute. Instead, Rutherford B. Hayes took office at the expense of Black rights in the South, as Reconstruction was ended as part of the resulting compromise. Pictured here and below: Counting the votes.

number of representatives each slave-holding state would be allowed in Congress. Were the Southern states to agree to a popular vote of only free citizens as the mode to determine the president, it would have been much more difficult for any Southerner after the overwhelmingly popular George Washington to be elected. (In fact, four of the first five American presidents came from Virginia, the state with the largest number of slaves in the 18th century.)

And so, once again, the convention sought a solution that would mollify the slave-holding states and enlist their support for the emerging Constitution. The

result was what we now know as the Electoral College, although that term was not used until the 19th century. The somewhat convoluted system called for each of the states to select "electors," whose sole purpose would be to choose the president, with a candidate needing to get a majority of the electoral votes to win. Absent that, the election would be decided by the House of Representatives. (Many delegates, failing to anticipate the growth of political parties, believed that most elections would end up in the House because multiple candidates would run, thereby splitting the vote and making a majority impossible for any candidate to achieve.) The number of electors assigned to each state would be based on the size of its congressional delegation (representatives in the House of Representatives plus two senators per state), thereby reinforcing the impact of the three-fifths compromise and giving the Southern states more influence in the presidential selection process.

But slavery was hardly the only factor. Three other arguments carried considerable weight. First, there were the concerns of many of the smaller states like New Jersey and Connecticut, who supported the system because they believed that the Electoral College—with two senators (and hence two electors) granted to each state regardless of size—would help level the playing field against larger states. Second, there was the position, argued forcefully by Alexander Hamilton, that a method needed to be devised to create a system of electors who would be elite patriots immune to the presumably fickle and unreliable sentiments of the masses. In this he reflected a common concern among the largely patrician founders about "mob rule." Finally, there was the widespread belief among many delegates that the vast majority of the populace was simply too ill-informed to make an intelligent decision about who should occupy the nation's highest office. Partly due to this concern, in the early years of our republic, there was no popular voting for president at all; the electors were mostly selected by state legislatures. It was not until the election of 1824, when 18 of 24 states selected their electors based on a popular vote for president, that individual voting became critically important.

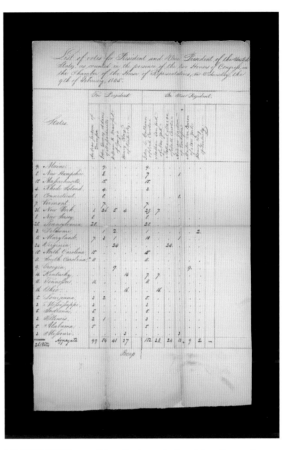

NO WINNER No candidate had a majority of the electoral votes in the 1824 race; John Quincy Adams went on to become president even though Andrew Jackson had more votes.

Our current winner-take-all arrangement, in which all of a state's electoral votes go to the candidate with the highest number of popular votes in the state, also took several decades to become standard. It became almost immediately universal, as dominant political parties in each state wanted to ensure that their preferred candidate would get all of their state's electoral votes. (Maine and Nebraska are the current outliers, with a hybrid system in which two electors—corresponding to each state's two senators—go to the statewide winning candidate and one elector is awarded to the winning candidate in each of the states' congressional districts.)

BOXED IN The official votes from the electors are carried through the halls of Congress on their way to be tallied in front of the House of Representatives and Senate.

A system of electors seemed a reasonable compromise to keep the Southern states in the fold, protect the country from mob rule and guarantee that those selecting the president were well-educated, civic-minded citizens. As with many other constitutional provisions, the Founders could not have anticipated the manner in which political practice evolved in the centuries since 1787. Five times in American history—twice in the last six elections—the winner of the popular vote has failed to be elected president. The first instance was in the 1824 election, which went as the delegates had anticipated many elections would, with multiple candidates splitting the vote and none achieving a majority in the Electoral College, the result being that the election was thrown to the House of Representatives. John Quincy Adams managed to prevail, largely, many believe, because of a deal he made to appoint Henry Clay, the fourth-place finisher in the election, as Secretary of State. Andrew Jackson, who would storm back to victory in 1828, had received 152,901 votes in the general election, well ahead of Adams' 114,023.

The agreement that elevated Republican Rutherford B. Hayes to the presidency in 1876, despite finishing with about 250,000 votes less than Democrat Samuel Tilden, was surely one of the more heinous bargains in American history. In exchange for the 20 disputed electoral votes that gave Hayes the victory, Republicans agreed to the removal of all federal troops in the South, thereby effectively ending Reconstruction and enabling Southern Democrats to institute the system of Jim Crow that barred African Americans from any meaningful participation in public life. It would be nearly 90 years before the nation would begin to address this fundamental inequity set in motion in 1876.

The winner of the popular vote lost three more times in the intervening years: Grover Cleveland lost handily in the Electoral College (233–168) to Benjamin Harrison in 1888, despite besting Harrison by more than 90,000 in the popular vote; in 2000, Al Gore beat George Bush by 0.51% in the popular vote but lost in the Electoral College after an extended dispute over the razor-thin results in Florida; and in 2016, Donald Trump defeated Hillary Clinton 304–227 in the Electoral College despite Clinton's beating Trump by nearly 3 million votes and 2.1% in the popular vote. In all of these, the outsize influence of so-called "swing states" engendered considerable criticism. In 2016, a total of fewer than 80,000 votes cast out of nearly 130 million nationwide produced victories for Trump in the three states—Pennsylvania, Michigan and Wisconsin—that put him over the top in the Electoral College vote.

The undue importance of a few states is a result of the Electoral College's emphasis on state, rather than national, totals, the upshot being that the only places that matter every four years are those states where the two parties are competitive. A vast swath of the electorate is barely addressed in general election campaigns because the results in their states are never in question. The Democratic candidate will always win New York, California and about a dozen other populous states; the Republican nominee will win Alabama, Louisiana, Nebraska, Kansas and about 15 less-populous states. That makes about 30 states whose citizens play essentially no role in the election of the president.

MAKING A CHANGE?

An Innovative Solution

On Feb. 26, 2006, a group that included prominent political reformers and former members of Congress held a press conference to announce its support for an innovative idea known as the National Popular Vote Interstate Compact (NPVIC). The plan proposes that states agree to cast all their electoral votes for the presidential candidate receiving the most popular votes nationally, regardless of the vote in their individual states. The compact would not take effect until enough states endorsed the plan to ensure the 270 electoral votes needed to guarantee victory for the popular vote winner.

Despite initial skepticism, legislation to enact the plan has been introduced in all 50 states and the District of Columbia; as of early 2021, the NPVIC has been adopted by 15 states and the District of Columbia, representing a total of 198 electoral votes. That's an impressive figure, but the remaining 72 electoral votes needed to put the plan into action may be very difficult to get. Thus far, all the states adopting the idea have been solid blue bastions of Democratic power, a reflection of the widespread belief that a popular-vote system favors the Democratic candidate.

Might enough current swing states—sometimes called purple states—become sufficiently blue to produce the 72 additional electoral votes needed? Texas (38 electoral votes), Pennsylvania (20) and Georgia (16) would do it; throw in North Carolina (15), Arizona (11), Nevada (6), Virginia (13) and Maine (4) as other possible states that might one day support the NPVIC. Without Texas moving in favor, the math becomes more difficult; the remaining states above represent 85 electoral votes, so the compact would need almost all of them.

One lingering question is whether a state that votes to endorse the plan might not later simply secede from the compact, thereby endangering the entire system, if political conditions in their state shift back toward Republican red. Supporters believe—or hope, anyway—that a vote to negate the will of the national majority might simply be too unpopular, even with many Republican voters, to succeed. We are probably years away from the NPVIC becoming effective, if it ever does, but it remains the nation's best hope for reform.

YAY OR NAY? New efforts are underway to create a popular-vote system.

There are arguments for and against this system. Critics emphasize the fundamental principle of one person/one vote, maintaining that there is something inherently inequitable in a system that makes a vote in New York or Indiana matter less than a vote in Pennsylvania or Wisconsin. In virtually every other nation in the world where elections are held, these critics note, the winner of the national popular vote is declared the victor in the election. Why should America be any different? The answer, according to the defenders of the Electoral College, is that the framers of the Constitution never intended one person/one vote to be the single overriding factor in determining the selection of the president. From the very beginning, they intended for smaller states to be given disproportionate influence as sovereign entities entitled to equal weight with other states regardless of their population. (For example: There is one senator for approximately every 19 million Californians, and one for every 290,000 citizens of Wyoming.) The framers were quite intentional in creating such a system, though one can debate whether they could ever have envisioned our largest state being 65 times more populous than our smallest. The critics answer that the concerns about state sovereignty are simply outdated; the interests of the smaller states are amply represented in Congress, without there being any need to employ an indirect method of presidential selection that has been shown to produce results contrary to the will of a majority of Americans. And in fact, 61% of all Americans support the abolition of the Electoral College, according to a 2020 Gallup poll.

These arguments are likely to rage on because, practically speaking, it is hard to envision a way that the Constitution could be amended to eliminate the Electoral College. The first, and biggest, hurdle would be Congress, which would have to pass, by a two-thirds majority in both the House and Senate, any proposed amendment before it could be sent to the states for ratification. Given that Democrats have won seven of the last eight popular votes for president—the one exception was George Bush's defeat of John Kerry in 2004 by 2.4%—there is no scenario in which Republicans, any Republicans, no less the number

HOLDING OFFICE After the 2012 election, then-Vice President Joe Biden handed the certificate of the Electoral College vote for Ohio back to Rep. Candice Miller.

that would be needed to produce the necessary two-thirds majority, would vote for such a measure. Even if every Democrat voted for the amendment in today's Congress, some 65 House Republicans and 17 Senate Republicans would be needed to achieve its successful passage. And that is before we even consider the likelihood of the amendment being passed in 34 state legislatures, which would represent the three-quarters majority needed to make the amendment law. (The same 34 votes would be needed to call a constitutional convention, the only other somewhat antiquated method the Constitution provides for amendments. That is even less conceivable.)

So the system survives, captive for the moment to the same deep partisan divide that typifies so much of our national politics today. Since it is likely to remain so for at least the foreseeable future, we can only hope that our national elections revert back to the historical norm, with very few elections taking place in which the Electoral College result differs from the popular vote. ★

ALEXANDER HAMILTON

The Federalist

Hamilton's advocacy of a strong central government helped establish America's financial system.

AMERICA HAS LONG BEEN PLEASED TO VIEW itself as a land where anyone can rise from humble beginnings and be a success. This has sometimes been true; sometimes not. But in the formative years of the republic, before class stratification became a fact of American life, such a rags-to-riches trajectory was perhaps more possible than at any time in our history. Many of the Founding Fathers came from an emerging aristocracy, but that was hardly the case with Alexander Hamilton, who illustrated the opportunities for advancement more vividly than any other member of the revolutionary generation. Born to a mother who was not married to his father, abandoned by that father at the age of 10, then cast adrift, along with his slightly older brother, by the death of his mother three years later, Hamilton was, in the parlance of the day, both a bastard and essentially an orphan by the age of 13.

All this took place in the hothouse environment of the British West Indies, teeming with a combustible mix of pirates and sugar barons, enterprising merchants and downtrodden slaves. Young Alexander learned early on to live by his wits and carefully curry favor with the rich and powerful who might help him advance. At the age of 14—or possibly 12; no one is really sure of the year of his birth—he began working as a merchant's clerk and living with the Stevens family on the island of St. Croix, now a part of the U.S. Virgin Islands. The boy was clever, ambitious and largely self-educated, eagerly grasping for every opportunity to learn and grow. He quickly displayed a propensity for writing, composing a vivid account of a hurricane that swept

HISTORIC KEEPSAKE
This gold "mourning ring," with a double shank band and a central square, included a braided lock of Hamilton's hair. It was given to a friend by Hamilton's widow, Eliza, in 1805, a year after his death.

"Men are rather reasoning than reasonable animals, for the most part governed by the impulse of passion."

ALEXANDER HAMILTON

across the island when he was 15 or 17. Published by the local paper, it described "the roaring of the sea and wind—fiery meteors flying about in the air—the prodigious glare of almost perpetual lightning—the crash of the falling houses—and the ear-piercing shrieks of the distressed." The prose may have been a touch purple, but it was vivid enough to persuade a group of

TWO ISLANDS, WORLDS APART Hamilton was born in Nevis, an island in the British West Indies, near the sugar plantation pictured above. Slavery was widespread on the islands at the time, essential to the grueling work of harvesting the sugarcane that was the primary source of revenue. Much of New York City, as shown by a 1776 map of lower Manhattan (opposite), was still farmland when Hamilton arrived there at the age of 18.

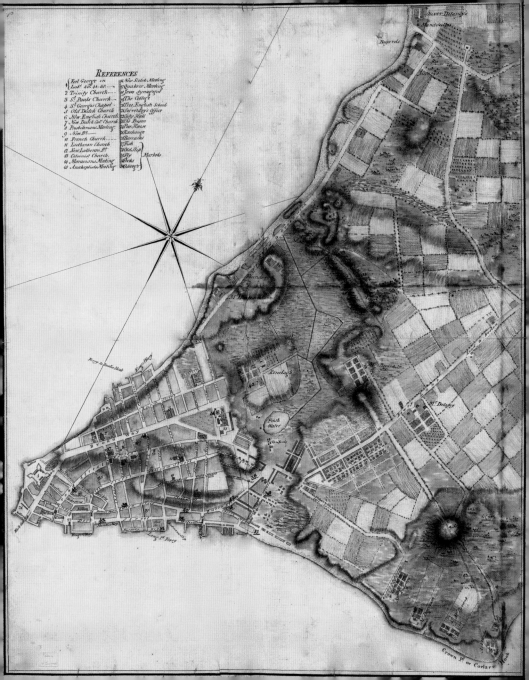

REFERENCES

1 Fort George in
  Lat.º 40.º 41.50'
2 Trinity Church
3 S.t Pauls Church
4 S.t Georges Chapel
5 Old Dutch Church
6 New English Church
7 New Dutch Cal. Church
8 Presbiterians Meeting
9 New B.ª
10 French Church
11 Lutheran Church
12 New Lutheran B.
13 Calvinist Church
14 Moravians Meeting
15 Anabaptists Meeting

16 New Scotch Meeting
17 Quakers Meeting
18 Jews Synagogue
19 The College
20 Free English School
21 Recorders Office
22 City Hall
23 The Prison
24 Poor House
25 Exchange
26 Barracks
27 Fish
28 Old Slip
29 Fly   Markets
30 Oswego

Manhattoes

Bayards

Kipsbergh

M.r Delancey

Crown P.t or Corlar's Hook

"...en the sword is once drawn,
...passions of men observe no
...nds of moderation."

EXANDER HAMILTON

local citizens to pool their funds and send the boy off to college in 1773 to Columbia—or King's College, as it was then known—in New York City.

INTO THE FRAY

Hamilton, now 18 or so, became an almost immediate proponent for the patriot cause. At a rally that followed the Boston Tea Party, just months after his arrival in New York, he made an impassioned speech urging his listeners to resist the oppressive tax policies of the British; otherwise "fraud, power and the most odious oppression will rise triumphant over right justice, social happiness and freedom." The speech earned him attention; the pamphlets that he wrote over the next two years burnished his image even further. When fighting broke out in 1775, he was eager to get into the battle despite his slight stature—he was 5-foot-7 and slim—and his youth. In March 1776, drawing on his friendship with influential members of the New York Legislature, he was commissioned as a captain of an artillery company, quickly establishing himself as a capable and unusually brave commander. In the darkest days of the war in late 1776, he caught the attention of Gen. George Washington with his bravery during the American retreat from Manhattan—Hamilton was one of the last to leave—and then in Princeton in early 1777 after Washington's daring foray across the Delaware. In late January, Washington offered him the position of aide-de-camp, and although Hamilton was too smart and ambitious to turn it down, he longed to return to the battlefield with his own company. Despite Hamilton's initial hesitation about accepting the job, his alliance with Washington was, without question, the most important relationship in his life, placing him as it did in the very center of the action, where decisions were made, policy was set and plans were pursued. For his part, Washington came to view Hamilton as a sort of son, relying mightily on his intelligence and skill.

KEY VICTORY On Jan. 3, 1777, Hamilton fought in the Battle of Princeton, which saw George Washington rally retreating American forces for an assault on the British, who were defeated and driven out of southern New Jersey. The victory bolstered sagging American morale.

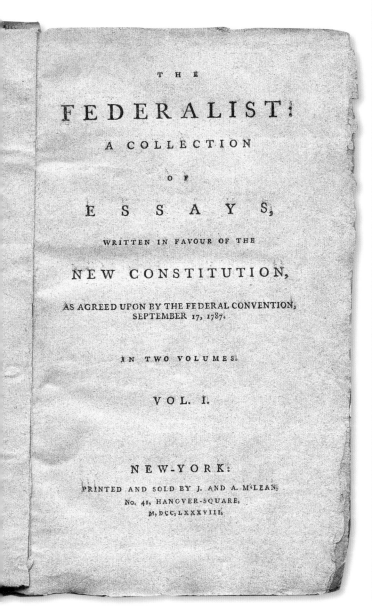

MAKING THE CASE Seventy-seven of *The Federalist* essays were initially distributed in newspapers, beginning in New York City, and then in news outlets throughout the colonies. Eight more essays were added after printers began combining them into volumes, like the one above, which was published in the critical year of 1788.

Hamilton would eventually write much of Washington's correspondence, negotiate on his behalf, and more than once even substitute his own judgment for that of his master. It was a pattern that would be repeated when he served as America's first secretary of the treasury in President Washington's cabinet.

In 1780, in the midst of the war, Hamilton married Elizabeth (often called Eliza) Schuyler, the daughter of a prominent New York family, a move that enhanced his status and wealth, two goals that his enemies—and a few historians—viewed as the primary reasons for the union. But the pair had eight children and their marriage appeared a happy one until Hamilton's untimely death 24 years later. (For more on Elizabeth Hamilton, see page 172.)

Still, Hamilton pined for combat and in early 1781 he quit Washington's staff and persuaded the general to allow him to return to battle. By that time, he had

CAPITOL IDEA
The first version of the Capitol Building was completed in 1800, but a separate wing for the House of Representatives was not constructed until 1811. The building's distinctive central dome and rotunda were added after the structure was partially burned by the British in 1814.

"The Constitution should consist only of general provisions; the reason is that they must necessarily be permanent, and that they cannot calculate for the possible change of things."

ALEXANDER HAMILTON

come to question the talents of his mentor as well as their emotional compatibility. "For three years past, I have felt no friendship for him," he wrote to a friend, "and have professed none. The truth is our own dispositions are the opposites of each other." Indeed they were: Washington was stoic, emotionally secure and impervious to criticism; Hamilton was volatile, thin-skinned, sometimes vindictive. By the time Hamilton returned to the field, the war was nearing its end, though it provided him with one last chance to display his bravery: At Yorktown, where his light infantry led a daring nighttime bayonet charge against one of two British strongholds, his victory helped pave the way for the final defeat of the British soon thereafter.

SHAPING HIS NATION

Hamilton's greatest contribution to the American story came after the war, of course. In 1787, he attended the Constitutional Convention in Philadelphia as an unapologetic nationalist, immovable in his conviction that a strong central, or federal, government was essential to the creation of a cohesive nation. "I fear that we shall let slip the golden opportunity of rescuing the American empire from disunion, anarchy and misery," he wrote to Washington. In his view, a critical first step in cementing the union was establishing the ability of the new federal government to raise revenue—"permanent and adequate funds to operate generally throughout the United States, to be collected by Congress," as he described it. At the convention, he proposed a system in which the central government would have almost unlimited powers over the states, a plan that stood almost no chance of passage, given the desire of a significant number of state delegates to retain some local control over their affairs. In the end, he supported the Constitution as written, with its careful delineation of powers between the three branches of government and between the national government and its constituent states.

While the American experiment is often presented as the inevitable triumph of an unstoppable idea, there were several moments—such as the period immediately after the Constitutional Convention—when events might have conspired to doom the young nation before it got started. All the brilliance and fundamental wisdom so evident in the delegates' work would have gone for naught if the Constitution failed to be ratified by the states. More than any other American, Hamilton enabled the Constitution to succeed.

According to Eliza Hamilton, the idea came to him while sailing in an elegant sloop on the Hudson River. What better way to support the efforts for ratification than to publish an extended series of essays praising the merits of the Constitution and addressing every possible

"Why has government been instituted at all? Because the passions of man will not conform to the dictates of reason and justice without constraint."
ALEXANDER HAMILTON

objection to it? To assist him, he recruited James Madison of Virginia and fellow New Yorker John Jay to share the writing, although in the end Hamilton himself wrote 51 of the 85 essays. The essays would come to be known as *The Federalist* or, more recently, *The Federalist Papers*. They appeared in newspapers between October 1787 and May 1788 and had a huge impact in swaying states to ratify the Constitution. They offered powerful arguments on behalf of the three proposed branches of government (executive, legislative and judicial), a bicameral legislature (the Senate and House of Representatives), and the vital concept of judicial review, which gave the Supreme Court the power to review acts of the legislature and void them if the court deemed them contrary to the Constitution. New York remained opposed, but partly through sheer force of will, Hamilton managed to get New York to vote for it at the state's ratifying convention in June 1788.

INFLUENCE IN OFFICE

Hamilton would continue to press for a strong federal government in his role as secretary of the treasury—America's first and arguably its most powerful—during the administration of Washington. First, he negotiated the Compromise of 1790. Thomas Jefferson and his Anti-Federalist allies would soon organize themselves

CELEBRATING THE CONSTITUTION Although only nine of the 13 states needed to ratify the Constitution for it to take effect, if New York was not on board, it was doomed to fail. It took all of Hamilton's persuasive powers to get the state's representatives to agree. At left, a parade commemorates the signing.

IN MEMORIAM
Elizabeth (Eliza) Hamilton fiercely protected her husband's legacy after his death, gathering a comprehensive collection of Hamilton's papers for publication. Author Ron Chernow (whose biography of Hamilton became the impetus for the smash musical that opened in 2015) noted the papers made it significantly easier to research Hamilton's life and achievements.

into the Republican (later Democratic-Republican) Party, but agreed to allow the national government to assume the war debts of the states and impose a federal system of taxes to cover the costs. Jefferson and the Virginians got an agreement from Hamilton to locate the nation's capital on the banks of the Potomac rather than in one of the Northern commercial centers like New York. For Hamilton, the compromise was essential in establishing the financial strength of the federal government and its capacity to raise the funds it needed. It had the added benefit of enlisting the support of America's wealthy merchant class for the young nation by selling revenue-raising bonds to its most well-heeled members. Soon thereafter, he proposed and succeeded in persuading Congress to pass the charter for a national bank, another critical tool in buttressing a powerful central government. In the process, he enunciated and popularized the fundamental principle that the national government had a critical role in support of the U.S. economy.

"There is a certain enthusiasm in liberty, that makes human nature rise above itself, in acts of bravery and heroism."

ALEXANDER HAMILTON

The final decade of Hamilton's life was full of conflict and intrigue. His behind-the-scenes machinations served to alienate almost everyone in politics at one point or another. John Adams came to detest him; Jefferson viewed him as too ambitious and unprincipled. Only Washington, ever the calm center in the midst of every storm, continued to recognize the brilliance of his young but impulsive protégé. But when Washington left the scene—Hamilton is said to have written much of his famous Farewell Address—Hamilton's only reliable ally was gone. The arguments persisted; the two great but contrary American impulses for and against a strong national government congealed into opposing political parties, and Hamilton continued to be surrounded by enemies. In 1804, he was killed by Aaron Burr, his most implacable nemesis. Hamilton was not yet 50. It is impossible to know what his contributions might have been in the decades to come, but his imprint on our American system of government remains unmistakable even today. ★

THE DUEL

A Gentleman's Solution

O n July 11, 1804, in an otherwise empty field in Weehawken, New Jersey, Aaron Burr, the sitting vice president of the United States, and Alexander Hamilton, the nation's first secretary of the treasury, stood facing each other with pistols at their sides at a distance of 10 paces. Each man, accompanied by his "second"—usually considered a friend and confidant—had departed at 5 a.m. from separate docks in Manhattan for the trip across the Hudson River in rowboats propelled by four oarsmen. Burr arrived first, along with his second, federal judge William Van Ness, at 6:30 a.m.; Hamilton and his second, Georgia district court judge Nathaniel Pendleton, arrived about 30 minutes later. Hamilton also brought Dr. David Hosack with him, in case he might find himself in need of medical attention. The seconds performed their assigned functions, which included inspecting the identical flintlock pistols

each man was carrying and establishing the proper distance between the two men.

What happened next remains less than entirely clear, but this much we know: Hamilton fired and missed; Burr did not miss—his bullet pierced Hamilton's abdomen, fractured a rib, ripped through his liver and lodged in his spine. Pendleton and Hosack quickly spirited Hamilton away, but nothing could be done; one of America's brightest lights was dead 31 hours later. The seconds offered differing accounts after the fact as to who fired first, whether Hamilton missed on purpose—his friends claimed that he had told them his intention to do so—or whether he shot wide involuntarily after being hit by Burr.

How could such a barbaric event even take place? Shocking as it may be to modern readers, duels—although illegal in many states—were not uncommon at the time; defeated political candidates, in particular, often issued challenges to their opponents as a means to reestablish their integrity and courage with the public. In the vast majority of cases, these contests did not result in death—most politicians were smart enough to know that the challenge was the key and that killing their opponent, particularly if he had just been elected to office by the voters, was not likely to enhance their popularity. Furthermore, most such disputes, known in the day as "affairs of honor," did not even get to the point of actual violence, as a ritualized process for settling them

DEADLY MEETING Burr (near right) and Hamilton (far right) were bitter enemies by the time they met in Weehawken. This set of dueling pistols (left) belonged to Rufus King, a U.S. senator from New York and a signer of the U.S. Constitution. The flintlock pistols are similar to the pair employed by Burr and Hamilton in their famous confrontation.

"But this much is known; Hamilton shot into the trees. Burr, leveling his pistol at his foe, did not."

AUTHOR PAUL COLLINS,
DUEL WITH THE DEVIL

through a series of letters normally resulted in a face-saving settlement for both potential combatants.

In the case of Burr and Hamilton, the blood was simply too bad—there had been too many insults and indignities, too much raw hatred—for the normal resolution process to succeed. The immediate cause of Burr's ire was Hamilton's behind-the-scenes manipulations to defeat Burr in his campaign for governor of New York in 1804, first blocking Burr from gaining the nomination from the Federalists—Burr had switched parties in an effort to get it—and then disparaging him during the general election that followed, in which Burr ran as an independent. During the campaign, a letter was published in which a Dr. Charles Cooper claimed to have had a conversation with Hamilton in which Hamilton described Burr as "a dangerous man" and went further, according to Cooper, offering an even "more despicable opinion" of Burr. The word "despicable" was apparently the trigger that set Burr off, although surely his challenge was based on a range of offenses extending back for years, including destroying Burr's hopes for the presidency in 1800. Burr demanded a denial from Hamilton of the claims in Cooper's letter; Hamilton refused to comply, leaving a duel as the only means for both men to retain their "honor."

FACING OFF The depiction at left presents the combatants as much closer to one another than they surely were—convention called for there to be 10 paces between them.

SAMUEL ADAMS

The Rabble-Rouser

The dedicated Bostonian used his gift for oratory to convince Americans to fight against taxation without representation.

A PASSIONATE POLITICIAN AND, ACCORDING TO some, a master propagandist, Samuel Adams used his skills early and often to sway his fellow Bostonians and eventually all Americans that the fight for separation from Britain was just and necessary. Raised in a prominent Puritan family, he took to public service at a young age and never stopped fighting for what he believed in, especially the clarion call for the American Revolution: "No taxation without representation." His early promotion of independence paved the way for the Boston Tea Party and the war itself. An original signer of the Declaration of Independence, he held both state and national offices, eventually becoming the governor of Massachusetts. The second cousin of President John Adams, Samuel was no less influential as one of the most important Founding Fathers of the new United States.

Born in Boston in 1722, Adams was one of 12 children, only three of whom lived past their third birthday. His father, Samuel Adams Sr., was a merchant and influential church deacon who held several political offices, including in the Massachusetts House of Representatives. The father's political dealings and involvement in a banking controversy likely influenced the young man's resistance to Britain's power over the colonies. In 1741, the British Parliament shut down the "land bank"—which supported colonials through mortgages—leaving the directors, including Adams Sr., personally liable for the loss.

Adams Jr. graduated from Harvard in 1743, but didn't immediately fall into politics. Rather, he kicked around Boston trying to find his

PUSHED TOO FAR After the British Parliament passed the Tea Act, which forced colonists to buy tea only from the British East India Company, Samuel Adams helped organize protests to prevent the tea shipments from ever reaching the Boston docks.

"The truth is, all might be free if they valued freedom, and defended it as they ought."

SAMUEL ADAMS

niche. He was too distracted by his political interests to be a dedicated banker as he worked at Thomas Cushing's counting house. And though his father lent him money to go into business himself, he lent half the money to a friend who didn't repay it. His father then gave him a job in the family's malt house that produced the malt needed to brew beer. (Although Samuel Adams Boston Lager, a brand started in 1985, holds his name, Adams likely wasn't a brewer.) For a while, he also worked as a lackadaisical tax collector. Adams' failure in business led historian Pauline Maier, author of *The Old Revolutionaries: Political Lives in the Age of Samuel Adams*, to write that he was "a man utterly uninterested in either making or possessing money."

He was entirely interested in politics, however, and his public career ignited in 1748 when he began writing essays for *The Independent Advertiser*, a publication he launched with friends in opposition to British naval impressment of colonials. He began to find his voice for agitation and independence, arguing that people should resist any encroachment on their constitutional rights. "The truth is all might be free," he wrote, "if they valued freedom and defended it as they ought."

Just as the younger Adams was hitting his stride, his father died, leaving his son to manage the family's estate, and the following year Adams married his pastor's daughter, Elizabeth Checkley; they would have six children, two of whom survived.

He worked his way up in local Boston politics until, in the 1760s, England's Parliament passed a series of acts aimed at taxing the colonists. Adams' response turned him into a figure to reckon with. As an elected official, he opposed the Sugar Act, arguing, "If Taxes are laid upon us in any shape without our having a legal Representation where they are laid, are we not reduced from the Character of free Subjects to the miserable State of tributary Slaves?" Adams' urging to resist the taxation was published widely and Massachusetts adopted his suggestions, giving him wider recognition as a leader in the emerging independence movement.

Britain then passed the Stamp Act and the Townshend Acts in what became a trade war, and Adams'

"The liberties of our country, the freedom of our civil constitution, are worth defending against all hazards: And it is our duty to defend them against all attacks."

SAMUEL ADAMS

response was to organize the Sons of Liberty, opposition groups in North and South Boston who took their anger to the streets, although historians differ as to whether he was behind the riots that followed. Some historians now believe Adams preferred petitions, boycotts and peaceful demonstrations to mob violence in fighting for his causes.

Nevertheless, resistance to the new taxes led to their repeal, and also to the royally appointed governor of Massachusetts to request military aid from England, which brought the British Army to Boston. Adams continued to write letters and essays in opposition to the British occupation, and was among the first to argue that "among the natural rights of the colonists are these: First the right to life, secondly to liberty, and thirdly to property; together with the right to defend them in the best manner they can."

In 1773, the British Parliament passed the Tea Act, designed to give the East India Company a monopoly on selling tea in the colonies; this threatened to put colonial merchants out of business. Adams again got to work organizing protests and boycotts, arguing that it was "the Duty of every American to oppose" the tax. While some have argued that Adams gave a signal to start the infamous Boston Tea Party, in which colonists boarded British ships and dumped the tea in the harbor, historians differ as to what role he actually played. Adams never revealed if he had gone to the wharf to watch the events unfold, but he wrote, "We cannot make events. Our business is wisely to improve them."

MORAL AUTHORITY Deeply religious, Adams was disappointed by what he considered to be a moral decay in the young country's values after the Revolution, earning the nickname "The Last Puritan" for his promotion of virtue in politics and society.

Adams next was elected to the First Continental Congress—a journey paid for by friends, who also chipped in to clothe the financially strapped Adams in finer suits. Over the next few years he moved back and forth between Boston and Philadelphia, guiding both his local government and the national efforts toward independence. He likely had a hand in the creation of the first minutemen companies, and it was partly to warn Adams of the British wanting to arrest him that Paul Revere made his famous ride shortly after Redcoats fired the first shots of the Revolutionary War in Lexington and Concord in 1775.

After signing the Declaration of Independence, Adams addressed the Congress, saying, "Our union is now complete; our Constitution composed, established and approved. You are now the guardians of your own liberties." Thomas Jefferson noted the important role Adams played in setting the country on a path toward independence, saying, "If there was any [guide] to the Revolution, Samuel Adams was the man."

During the war, Adams served on various military committees and helped draft the Articles of Confederation. He also helped draft the Massachusetts constitution. By 1781, however, plagued by what is now believed to have been an essential tremor in his hands, which made writing difficult, Adams stepped down from the Continental Congress and returned home to Boston.

Still, he didn't retire. He went on to serve in the state senate and his efforts helped ensure Boston provided free public education for children, even for girls. And although Adams, a Jeffersonian Republican, was initially opposed to the new Constitution's idea of a central government and in favor of states rights, the addition of the Bill of Rights soothed his skepticism.

In 1789, Adams was elected lieutenant governor of Massachusetts and then served four annual terms as governor until, at age 74, he declined to run for reelection. Samuel Adams died in 1803. ★

"*Liberty may be endangered by the abuse of liberty, but also by the abuse of power.*"

JAMES MADISON

JAMES MADISON

The Builder

No American deserves more credit for the shape of the U.S. Constitution than Madison.

NONE OF THE FOUNDING FATHERS SEEMED LESS destined for greatness than James Madison. Truly tiny at 5-foot-4 and barely 100 pounds, he was sickly throughout his life—some historians believe he suffered from epilepsy—and extremely shy and uncomfortable in public settings. He was a hesitant speaker and much preferred conversation in small groups to the extended speechifying required by the congresses, conventions and rallies so typical of his nation's revolutionary period. Later, in his less than fully successful presidency—a job for which he was ill-suited—he was enormously fortunate to have his wife, Dolley Payne Todd, by his side, a woman whose outgoing charm and welcoming personality made her the antithesis of her withdrawn, standoffish husband. By the time Madison entered the White House in 1809, Dolley had already performed the role of first lady—although the term was not yet in common use—for the widowed Thomas Jefferson and was known throughout Washington as a gracious and entertaining hostess. If Dolley was in the room, guests could ignore the less-than-convivial Madison. Author Washington Irving, a frequent guest at the White House, described Dolley as "a fine portly, buxom dame, who has a smile and a pleasant word for everybody," while "Jemmy [nickname for James] Madison—ah poor Jemmy—he is but a withered little apple-john." (For more on Dolley Madison, see page 170.)

But despite the criticisms hurled at Madison later in life, no one ever denied his towering intellect or his indispensable contribution to the ingenious system of checks and balances that continues to govern

MAKING A POINT Quill pens, like the one above, were used for the writing—and signing—of the Declaration of Independence and the U.S. Constitution. The quills were usually taken from the wing feathers of a large bird such as a goose and then sharpened to a fine point for delicate writing, or to a broader point for thicker lettering on posters and handbills.

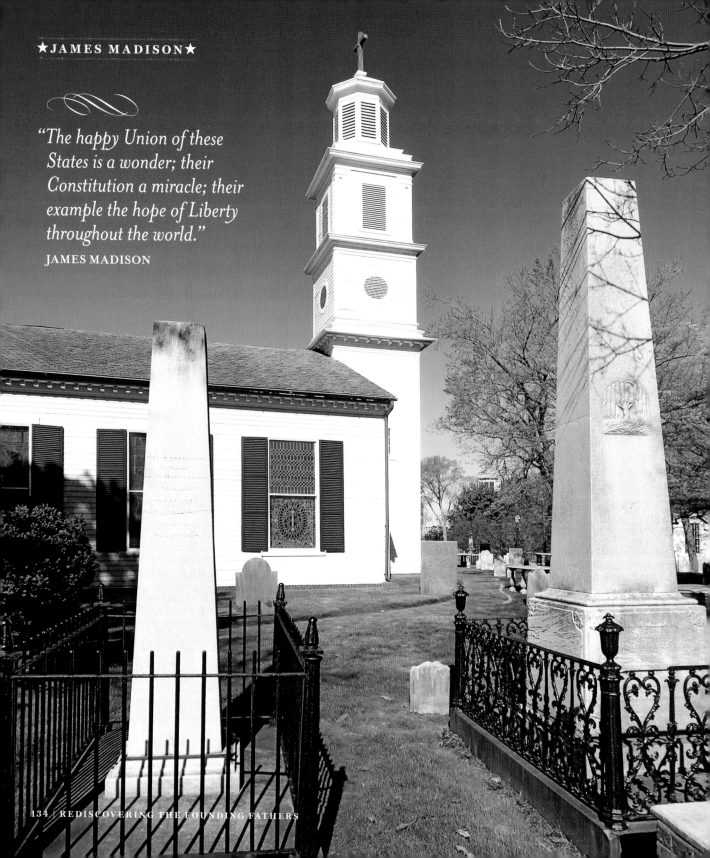

"The happy Union of these States is a wonder; their Constitution a miracle; their example the hope of Liberty throughout the world."

JAMES MADISON

A North-West Prospect of Nassau-Hall, with a Front View of the Presidents House, in New Jersey

America to this day. Historians have called him the Father of the Constitution and the title is well-deserved.

FINDING HIS VOICE

Madison was born in 1751, in the home he would occupy throughout his life, in Montpelier, Virginia, on the edge of the Blue Ridge Mountains. As the eldest son of one of Virginia's wealthiest and most established planter families, he would never have to worry about earning a living. He attended Princeton University—he completed his degree in two years—rather than the much closer College of William and Mary in Williamsburg because he considered the climate in eastern Virginia "unhealthy for persons going from a mountainous region" and the student life at William and Mary too

YOUNG PATRIOT Madison graduated from Princeton—the woodcut above shows Nassau Hall (left) and the university president's house—in 1771. During the Second Virginia Convention, Patrick Henry made his famous declaration of revolutionary fervor—"Give me liberty or give me death"—in St. John's Church (opposite page) in Richmond, Virginia, where the 1775 convention was held. Madison and Henry would later become enemies due to Henry's vehement opposition to Madison's belief in a strict separation of church and state.

dominated by parties and other unscholarly activities. After graduating from Princeton in 1771, he found himself uninspired by law or the clergy, the two most likely occupations for young men of his class. He also was not swept up in the revolutionary fervor that had been

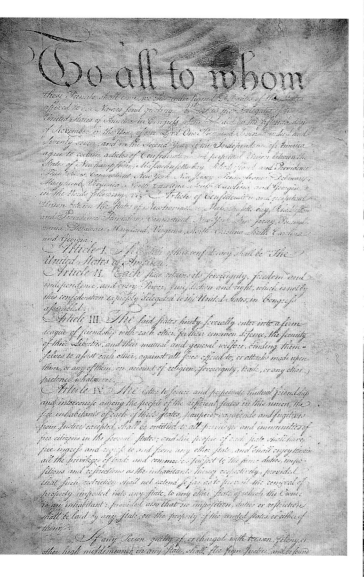

INSUFFICIENT MEASURE The Articles of Confederation (above) were drafted by a committee of the Second Continental Congress designated for the task on July 12, 1776. The resulting document was ratified by the states and took effect in 1781. Alas, the Articles proved woefully inadequate to the changing needs of the nation, mandating the drafting in 1787 of a new constitution, which was debated and approved in Independence Hall (right) in Philadelphia.

gripping the colonies in the 1760s and 1770s. Even the Boston Massacre (1770) and Tea Party (1773) failed to provoke a passionate response. He did rouse himself to write in condemnation of religious persecution in Virginia and to express his support for independence in 1774, but his energies were not fully engaged until 1776, when he was elected to the Fifth Virginia Convention and presented with the intellectual challenge of proposing a new form of state government to replace the now-defunct British system. His contributions were not as significant as those of elder statesmen like George Mason, but he did press for a subtle change in Mason's Virginia Declaration of Rights to stress the "full and free exercise of religion" as a fundamental right. Mason's document would function as a template for the Bill of Rights, added to the Constitution in 1791.

When the Revolutionary War began in 1775, Madison was forced to remain on the sidelines. "He was restrained from entering into the military service," Madison wrote of himself, "by the unsettled state of his health and the discouraging feebleness of his

EARLY SCHISM The first years of the republic saw a great divide between those who viewed America's future prosperity as dependent on growing cities like Philadelphia (right)—the largest urban area in the United States in 1790 with a population of 44,000 people—and those who thought the nation's destiny lay in its frontier regions (above), where Americans were just beginning to move in the years after the Revolutionary War. Madison and his great patron, Thomas Jefferson, were firmly in the latter camp. When the two men—Jefferson as president, Madison as secretary of state—learned that France was interested in selling a large chunk of its American holdings, they jumped at the chance, and the resulting Louisiana Purchase nearly doubled the nation's size and opened up vast new swaths of wilderness for American expansion.

constitution." But his involvement in the discussions surrounding the future shape of the "united states" continued to expand. He was elected to the Continental Congress in 1779, and then to the Confederation Congress, which began operating under the original Articles of Confederation after the war ended with

"Knowledge will forever govern ignorance; and a people who mean to be their own governors must arm themselves with the power which knowledge gives." JAMES MADISON

an American victory in 1781. Throughout this period, he became increasingly convinced that something much stronger than the Articles would be needed to bind the emerging states into a lasting union capable of raising money, settling disputes between the states and conducting foreign policy. In 1786, knowing that his own views in favor of a strong federal government were becoming well-known, he persuaded states-rights advocate John Tyler to call for a national convention to address issues of commerce affecting all the states. The resulting Annapolis Convention was poorly attended—only 12 delegates from five states showed up—but it did produce a call, strongly urged by Madison, for a broader convention the following spring to examine the very structure of the government itself.

BLUEPRINT FOR A NATION

By May 1787, when the Constitutional Convention (see page 54) gathered in Philadelphia, Madison had already articulated many of his fundamental principles in a widely distributed essay, "Vices of the Political System of the United States." His thinking in that document became the basis for the so-called Virginia Plan, which Madison presented to the assembled delegates at the beginning of the convention. Not every element of his scheme was included in the constitution that was hammered out over the next four months, but much of it was, and his essential insight that a balance of power needed to be maintained between the federal government and the states, and between the three branches of government he proposed, became the very bedrock of the U.S. Constitution. In achieving his aims, Madison did most

of his work behind the scenes in the small discussions he preferred. Contrary to his reputation in later life as a misanthrope, William Pierce of Georgia described him as "a Gentleman of great modesty—with a remarkable sweet temper. He is easy and unreserved among his acquaintants, and has a most agreeable style of conversation."

In 1788, as part of the campaign for constitutional ratification—nine of the original 13 states would need to approve it—Madison was happy to partner with Alexander Hamilton and John Jay in the writing of *The Federalist Papers*. While Hamilton authored most of the essays included in the collection, Madison composed several of the most influential, including *Federalist* essay No. 10, which eloquently presented the Constitution as possessing the ability to "break and control the violence of faction." (Howard Zinn, in his famously left-leaning *A People's History of the United States* (1980), argued that many of the Founding Fathers were just as concerned about potential violence from "propertyless" working-class Americans as they were about avoiding the oppressive British monarchical system.) The battle for ratification was hard-fought and the outcome was not assured until the end, but the Constitution became the law of the land. In June 1788, Madison's home state, Virginia, became the 10th state to ratify it.

But the Constitution remained at risk, with many opponents, including fellow Virginians Patrick Henry and George Mason. Madison knew that the Constitution would not be secure until a bill of rights was added to address the concerns of those who believed that individuals were not adequately protected from the potential depredations of a newly powerful federal government. As a member of the newly created House

LIFE AFTER PRESIDENCY After leaving office, Madison served as the head of the University of Virginia as well as a delegate to the Virginia Constitutional Convention in 1829. A lifelong slave owner, Madison was a founding member of the American Colonization Society, which advocated for a gradual abolition of slavery and resettlement of slaves in Africa.

MAKING THE CASE

The Federalist Papers

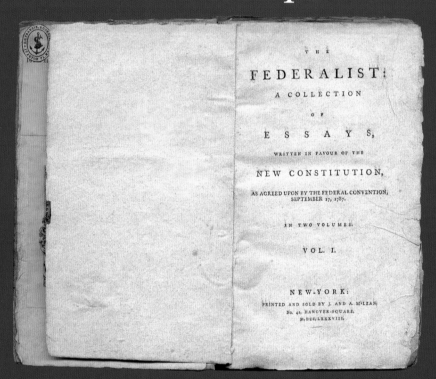

G iven that they were authored in haste and in the midst of a pitched political battle, it is astonishing how eloquent and beautifully written *The Federalist Papers* are, offering a timeless rationale for the uniquely American form of government embodied in the U.S. Constitution. Their creation was the brainchild of Alexander Hamilton, who emerged from the Constitutional Convention seeing a clear need to argue the case for ratification as widely as possible. He recruited Madison, whose intellect he had come to admire, and John Jay of New York, to assist him. They were given the task of writing a series of essays that would argue the strengths of the new Constitution and to answer every possible objection to it. (Gouverneur Morris of New York, who was heavily involved in the drafting of the Constitution— most famously its eloquent preamble—was also asked to participate, but declined to get involved, citing other obligations.)

The three men wrote a total of 85 essays, published first in newspapers in New York, and then across the country, from October 1787 to August 1788. All were written under the pseudonym Publius (a consul of the Roman Republic and one of four Roman aristocrats who overthrew the monarchy to establish a more democratic form of government in 509 B.C.) But word of the actual authors became widely known, and scholars have since identified Hamilton as the author of 51, Madison 29, and Jay five (he withdrew soon afterward, due to ill health).

In 1788, all the essays were published in book form as *The Federalist*. Madison offered one of the most trenchant justifications for the Constitution and its system of checks and balances in *Federalist* essay No. 50: "The aim of every political constitution is, or ought to be, first to obtain for rulers men who possess most wisdom to discern, and most virtue to pursue, the common good of the society; and in the next place, to take the most effectual precautions for keeping them virtuous whilst they continue to hold their public trust."

of Representatives, Madison sponsored the first 10 amendments to the Constitution, which became known as the Bill of Rights. The first amendment articulated the most important goals for Madison and Mason: "Congress shall make no law respecting an establishment of religion, or prohibiting the free exercise thereof; or abridging the freedom of speech, or of the press; or the right of the people peaceably to assemble, and to petition the Government for a redress of grievances." The ratification of the Bill of Rights in 1791 would not only protect the rights of individuals but also ensure the success of the Constitution as a whole.

DIVIDED NATION

Madison and Hamilton, allies early on in their support of the Constitution, would become opponents in the years that followed, as Madison would come to view the federalism advocated by Hamilton as empowering the

ODD COUPLE James and Dolley Madison (above) could not have been more different. While Dolley enjoyed being the center of attention at White House events, often dressing in flamboyant low-cut dresses, James liked to fade into the background, preferring to conduct his business in small groups. In spite of their differences, the couple by all accounts remained deeply devoted to each other.

central government with an authority not intended by the Constitution. He was joined in this view by Thomas Jefferson, and the two Virginians soon formed America's first political party, the Democratic-Republicans, to advance their mission to limit the power of the federal government. Madison would go on to achieve a mixed record as secretary of state under Jefferson and then as president from 1809 to 1817, but his legacy as the framer of his nation's constitution would survive long after the political squabbles of his day were forgotten. He died in 1836 at age 85 of heart failure. ★

One Nation

A key question the framers attempted to solve in the Constitution continues to this day: Does federal power trump that of the states?

BEFORE THE UNITED STATES BECAME "united," Americans saw themselves first and foremost as citizens of their individual states, rather than participants in a single unified nation. Given the fear of domination by another overbearing central government like the British monarchy, the issue of what powers the states would retain under the young country's new Constitution was a source of considerable debate. The Articles of Confederation, which defined the political structure before the Constitution, proposed a federal government with little power over the states. It was only as national leaders began to see the limitations of a state-dominated arrangement and the desperate need for a federal government capable of defending the nation, conducting foreign policy and settling disputes

between sometimes bickering states, that the move for a constitutional convention and the establishment of a strong federal government gained momentum.

The framers attempted to settle the question of the proper relationship between federal and state governments with the language of the so-called supremacy clause of the Constitution (Article VI, paragraph 2), which states: "This Constitution, and the Laws of the United States which shall be made in pursuance thereof; and all treaties made, or which shall be made, under the authority of the United States, shall be the supreme law of the land; and the judges in every state shall be bound thereby, anything in the constitution or laws of any state to the contrary notwithstanding." Alexander Hamilton, writing in the *Federalist Papers*,

THE BEGINNING OF A NEW ERA While the *Brown* decision only prohibited segregation in schools, it marked the start of desegregation in other areas, including libraries, transportation, restaurants and other public places.

further explained the concept: "But it will not follow from this doctrine that acts of the large society which are not pursuant to its constitutional powers, but which are invasions of the residuary authorities of the smaller societies, will become the supreme law of the land. These will be merely acts of usurpation, and will deserve to be treated as such." The logic seemed simple. Any law or action passed by Congress or taken by the federal government that is "pursuant" to the Constitution is binding on state as well as federal officials

SEPARATE AND UNEQUAL After the Supreme Court issued its landmark *Brown v. Board of Education* ruling, states were forced to desegregate their school systems.

and courts. But just what actions fall within that broad definition has been difficult to determine at times, a lack of clarity that has led to an ongoing struggle throughout the nation's history between those in favor of a strong federal government and those inclined to stress the right of the states to govern their own affairs.

The term "states' rights" has a checkered legacy. During the civil rights movement in the 1950s and '60s, white segregationists regularly invoked it to defend bigotry against Black Americans and to legitimize the system of Jim Crow throughout the South. "Segregation

MAKING A STAND Gov. George Wallace stood at the University of Alabama to denounce the enrollment of Black students.

now, segregation tomorrow, segregation forever," Alabama Gov. George Wallace famously declared in his inaugural speech in January 1963. Six months later, when he stood in front of the entrance to the University of Alabama to prevent Vivian Malone and James Hood from becoming the first African American students in the history of that institution, he justified his action on the basis that Alabama was a sovereign state entitled to run its educational institutions in any way it saw fit. "States' rights" became the rallying cry for racists throughout the South in their efforts to resist court-ordered integration and the deconstruction of Jim Crow.

Most Americans see that history of Southern resistance to Black participation in American life as

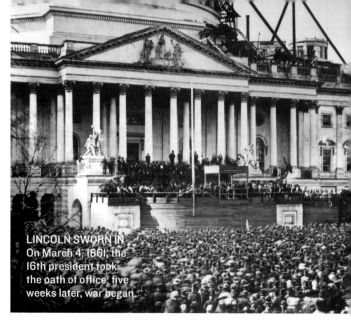

LINCOLN SWORN IN On March 4, 1861, the 16th president took the oath of office; five weeks later, war began.

OLD HICKORY FLEXES HIS MUSCLE President Andrew Jackson was determined to show the federal government's ultimate authority over state's rights.

despicable—as indeed it was—but those in support of states' rights were not always driven by bigotry. In 1798, the Federalists engineered the passage of the Alien and Sedition Acts, a series of measures that restricted immigration and gave the federal government considerable leeway in the detention of immigrants viewed as dangerous; it even declared speech by citizens critical of the government to be illegal, an act that today would surely be viewed as a clear violation of the First Amendment's right to free speech. Madison and Thomas Jefferson composed resolutions passed in Virginia and Kentucky declaring that states have the sovereign right to disregard or "nullify" legislation like the Alien and Sedition Acts, which in their view clearly extended federal power beyond its constitutional limits. With the defeat of the Federalists in the election of 1800 and Jefferson's ascent to the presidency, the Alien and Sedition Acts were largely eliminated, but the issue of states' rights and potential nullification—a tactic Madison would come to oppose—remained part of the national conversation.

A particular source of contention in the early 19th century was tariff and trade policy, which tended to favor one state over another. In 1832, South Carolina declared protective tariffs, favorable to the industrial North but detrimental to the agricultural South, to be null and void within the borders of South Carolina. President Andrew Jackson, a staunch proponent of a

Abraham Lincoln won the presidential election without any support from the Southern states, leading to talk of secession. Lincoln believed it to be his sacred duty to preserve the Union at all costs rather than allow the country to splinter apart.

BROTHER VS. BROTHER
Confederate Gen. Pierre
Gustave T. Beauregard had
trained at West Point under
Maj. Robert Anderson, the
commander at Fort Sumter,
whom he ultimately attacked.

strong federal government, responded by dispatching the U.S. Navy to the South Carolina coast to enforce the tariffs and assert federal authority over trade policy, ending the crisis in favor of the national government.

In the decades that followed, slavery—the issue festering within the body politic since the nation's founding—took center stage. Seven Southern states, viewing Abraham Lincoln as a dangerous threat to the institution of slavery they saw as essential to their economy, declared their intention to secede from the union

after Lincoln's election in 1860. South Carolina went so far as to declare Fort Sumter, which sat off its coast in Carolina Bay, to belong to the state rather than the federal government, an act of open rebellion that provoked the first shots fired in the Civil War. A horrifying total of 625,000 Americans would die in the carnage that followed before the Union's victory established once and for all that the United States is indissoluble, and no nation declaring itself committed to equal rights can tolerate the institution of slavery within its borders.

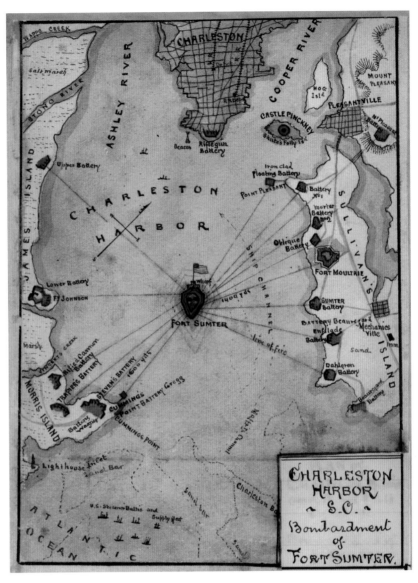

Today the resolution of most state/federal conflicts takes place in the courtroom. Over the decades, beginning with the landmark *Brown v. Board of Education* (1954) mandating integration, the Supreme Court has interpreted the due process and equal protection clauses of the 14th Amendment to apply to every state and its citizens, protecting legislation like the Civil Rights Act (1964) and the Voting Rights Act (1965). But a host of issues potentially pitting states against the federal government remain, including gay marriage,

OPENING SHOTS Early in the morning on April 12, 1861, Confederate forces began attacking Fort Sumter, a federal fort located in the Charleston, South Carolina, harbor. By the next day, the garrison commander surrendered and the American Civil War had begun.

marijuana legalization, capital punishment, assisted suicide and gun control. Should there be national legislation on any or all of these matters? Time will tell, but it's safe to assume that these will not be the last thorny questions to test the nation's federalist system. ★

> "This country and
> its people seem to
> have been made
> for each other."

JOHN JAY

JOHN JAY
The Legal Eagle

The first chief justice of the United States and a contributor to the *Federalist Papers*, Jay helped shape the new government.

A MODERATE FROM NEW YORK WHO BECAME THE nation's first chief justice, John Jay was intelligent, highly educated and measured in his thinking. Preferring patient examination of circumstances to impulsive action and always peace over war, he was slow to back America's separation from Britain, fearing the disruption it would cause to trade and the economy. But as British policies grew more antagonistic, his opinion changed and he became an ardent patriot and backer of the Revolutionary War. From that point on, Jay's was an important legal and diplomatic voice in America's early development as an independent nation.

Jay was born two days before Christmas, in 1745, to a wealthy merchant family in New York City. His father, who traded in furs, wheat and timber, retired shortly after Jay's birth, after two of his children were left blind by smallpox, and the family moved to Rye, New York. Mostly homeschooled, Jay entered King's College (now Columbia University) at 14 and became a law clerk upon graduation; he was admitted to the New York bar in 1768. In 1774, having established his own law practice, he married 17-year-old Sarah Livingston, the eldest daughter of the governor of New Jersey, which gave him entrée into rarefied colonial social circles and he began to turn his eye to politics.

Jay soon became a member of the New York Committee of Correspondence, a group that spoke out against British rule. Jay held a conservative view of the growing call for revolution, however, fearing the prospect of "mob rule" and damage to property rights. Upon being elected to the First Continental Congress that same year, Jay urged

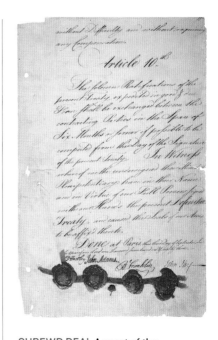

SHREWD DEAL As part of the negotiating team for the Treaty of Paris after the Revolutionary War, Jay helped secure all U.S. land east of the Mississippi River, with the exception of British territories in Canada and Spanish territory in Florida.

reconciliation with England's parliament, and the following year he helped draft the Olive Branch Petition.

But with the outbreak of the Revolutionary War, he evolved into a passionate patriot who ultimately urged separation from England and worked to sway New York toward the cause. In an open letter to the people of Great Britain, he argued, "we consider ourselves... as free as our fellow-subjects in Britain, and that no power on Earth has a right to take our property from us without our consent."

After helping to draft the Constitution of New York in 1777, he returned to the Continental Congress. Jay would become an important diplomat, and for his first posting, in 1779, he was appointed minister to Spain with the mandate to build support and financial aid for American independence. Though he did manage to raise funds, the royal Spanish court snubbed him.

From there, he traveled to Paris with his family (he and Sarah would have six children during their 28-year marriage), where they resided with Benjamin Franklin, with whom he was negotiating an end to the war in the colonies. Future president John Adams joined them, and the three hammered out a deal that resulted in the Treaty of Paris, ending the American Revolution in September 1783, after seven bloody years.

The time in Paris was especially difficult for Jay, whose father died while the negotiations were ongoing. The sixth of seven surviving siblings, Jay suddenly inherited responsibilities for his siblings, several of whom were disabled, including the blind Peter and Anna; another brother, Augustus, who was developmentally disabled; and sister Eve, who suffered from emotional issues. All of this—along with another brother, Frederick, who was often in financial straits—was no doubt distracting. Nevertheless, Adams lauded Jay's negotiating prowess, saying he was "of more importance than any of the rest of us," in achieving the peace deal.

Upon his return to America, Jay served as secretary of foreign affairs, the precursor to secretary of state. As he attempted to establish a durable American foreign policy—establishing territorial boundaries, seeking European recognition of American independence,

dealing with the country's war debts to European banks—he began to believe the new country needed a stronger constitution than the Articles of Confederation, and would require a strong central government.

With these ideas, he joined Alexander Hamilton and James Madison in urging a balanced system of government. Addressing the "People of the State of New York," Jay wrote five of what became known as the *Federalist Papers*. He saw fragility in the new country should the states remain without a unifying government.

One area of concern he recognized was slavery—though he had enslaved five people. He favored manumission, a policy of freeing the enslaved, and in 1785 founded the New York Manumission Society, which organized boycotts against businesses involved in the slave trade. "To contend for our own liberty, and to deny that blessing to others, involves an inconsistency not to be excused," he wrote.

After the Constitution was ratified in 1787, President Washington offered Jay a new job: chief justice of the United States. He accepted, and was instrumental in establishing the rules and procedures under which the Supreme Court would operate, including early precedent for political independence, despite Hamilton's failed effort to persuade the court to endorse legislation regarding the government assuming states' debts.

Over the next several years, Jay presided over the court and negotiated the Jay Treaty, ending English control of their Northwest forts and temporarily avoiding a war over grievances such as British impressment of American sailors. (The same issues would eventually lead to the War of 1812.) "Nations in general will make war whenever they have a prospect of getting anything by it," he lamented. The treaty was so unpopular, Jay reportedly joked he could travel at night from Boston to Philadelphia by the light of his burning effigies.

By 1801, after serving as the second governor of New York for six years, Jay declined further political offices and retired to his farm in New York, where his wife died a short while later. Jay continued to monitor and encourage the antislavery movement, and became president of the American Bible Association. He passed away in 1829 at the age of 83. ★

POPULAR DISCONTENT
Although 1795's Jay Treaty, with John Jay as chief negotiator, helped forestall another war with Great Britain, it was extremely unpopular and left many Democratic-Republican Party members fuming, with Jay's likeness hanged in effigy all across the country.

THE SUPREME COURT

Evolution of an Institution

As hard as it is for us to believe today, the Supreme Court was hardly "supreme" in its earliest iterations. Article III of the Constitution, which established it, consists of just three sections, far shorter than either Article I, which created Congress and delineated its powers, or Article II, which defined the role of the executive branch. Article III defined the Court's powers as extending "to all cases, in law and equity, arising under this Constitution, the laws of the United States, and treaties made, or which shall be made, under their authority." But criminal matters were left to state courts, and the framers, in further defining the role of the Court, suggested that its primary responsibility would be to settle disputes between the states and otherwise handle cases "affecting ambassadors, other public ministers and consuls" and "all cases of admiralty and maritime jurisdiction."

The Judiciary Act of 1789 called the Court into being, and all six of George Washington's nominees—the Court would fluctuate in size between five and 10 members until permanently settling at its current size of nine in 1869—were unanimously approved by the Senate. During its early years, the Court met in borrowed quarters in New York, Philadelphia and Washington as the nation's capital shifted location between 1789 and 1800. It was not until 1935 that the justices of the Supreme Court took up residence in a facility constructed specifically for them—the elegant neoclassical building in which they function to this day.

In its first year of existence, the Court, led by Chief Justice John Jay, spent much of its time on organizational matters. It did not hear a case—a minor

one at that—until August 1791, nearly a year and a half after its initial meeting. After Jay resigned as chief justice in 1795 (only four cases were heard during his tenure), he described the Court as lacking "the energy,

weight and dignity which are essential to its affording due support to the national government."

It was not until the towering figure of John Marshall, who became chief justice in 1801, that the Court began its journey toward the influential status that it enjoys today. Indeed, before the seminal *Marbury v. Madison* case, the Court's most fundamental duty—to review legislative acts of Congress and determine whether or not they were constitutional—had not yet been established. During his 34 years as chief justice—no one held the position longer—Marshall enhanced the power and influence of the Court in a host of ways, establishing the principle of judicial review in *Marbury* (1803), the authority of the Court over state action in *McCulloch v. Maryland* (1819), and the right of the federal government to regulate interstate commerce in *Gibbons v. Ogden* (1824). He also began the tradition of issuing a single opinion, written by just one justice—Marshall wrote two-thirds of the opinions of the Court on constitutional questions— further enhancing the sense of the court working as a powerful, unified body and speaking with one authoritative voice. Marshall's rulings not only enhanced the power of the court itself but they also established a nearly unassailable body of law supporting a broad conception of federal authority that we follow today.

EXPANDING INFLUENCE The Supreme Court's original jurisdiction extended only to the 13 states along the East Coast, as shown in shades of pink and brown on the map at right. Chief Justices John Jay (above left) and John Marshall (above right) were fundamental in establishing the primacy of the Court.

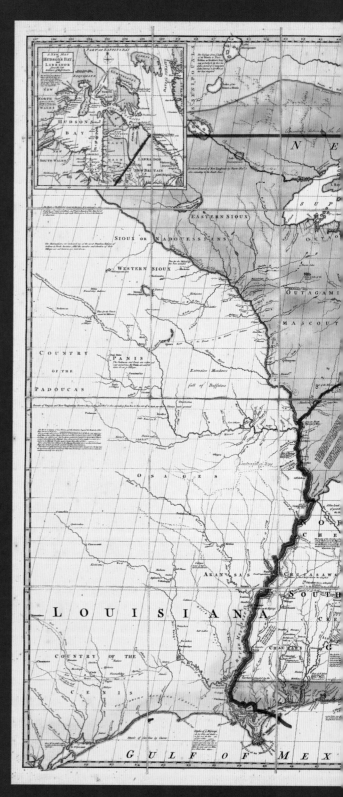

JAMES MONROE
The Forward-Thinking Leader

The experienced Monroe set forth the United States' first foreign policy establishing the country's authority.

SKILLFUL FOREIGN POLICY WAS A HALLMARK OF JAMES Monroe's presidency, which lasted from 1817–1825. His most recognizable achievement, the Monroe Doctrine, changed how America viewed the world, and how the rest of the world viewed America.

Based on the ideas of Secretary of State John Quincy Adams, the Doctrine states four key points: 1) the United States' political system is separate from the European system; 2) the U.S. will no longer be colonized by Europe; 3) the U.S. has the right to oppose any European colonization or recolonization of independent republics in the Americas; and 4) the U.S. will respect and not interfere in any and all established European colonies in the Americas nor will it become involved with Europe's domestic affairs or intervene in any European wars that do not impact the U.S. Monroe announced the new policy to Congress in his 1823 State of the Union address: "It is impossible that the allied powers should extend their political system to any portion of either continent without endangering our peace and happiness."

The fear of recolonization of Latin America by European monarchs led to wide support of the Monroe Doctrine, as it later became known, and of Monroe himself. Biographer Harry Ammon described him as having a "rare ability of putting men at ease by his courtesy, his lack of condescension, his frankness, and by what his contemporaries looked upon as his essential goodness and kindness of heart."

Future presidents, like Theodore Roosevelt, used the doctrine to enact various policies throughout the Americas, proving it to be a powerful and resilient tool of American foreign policy.

MAKING A STATEMENT A plaque at the James Monroe Museum and Memorial Library in Fredericksburg, Virginia, hails Monroe's most lasting legacy, which established U.S. sovereignty in the Western Hemisphere.

"National honor is the national property of the highest value."

JAMES MONROE

At the start of his presidency, Monroe, a Virginian who held two cabinet positions (secretary of war and secretary of state) at the same time under James Madison, filled his cabinet with members who were geographically spread out to ease political tension. While serving in his first term, Monroe went on a goodwill tour, traveling the country as far west as Michigan and the Missouri territory, as far north as Maine and south to Georgia and Kentucky. After visiting Boston along the tour, a Boston newspaper, the *Columbian Centinel*, proclaimed this was the "Era of Good Feelings," a term the nation soon got behind. ★

"Never did a government commence under auspices so favorable, nor ever was success so complete."

JAMES MONROE'S FIRST INAUGURAL ADDRESS, 1817

MONROE'S INAUGURATION

MAKING HISTORY
Cabinet members (seated, from left) John Quincy Adams, William Harris Crawford, William Wirt, John C. Calhoun, Daniel D. Tompkins and John McLean joined Monroe (standing) in establishing the historic doctrine that bears his name.

The Women Behind the Founding Fathers

Intelligent, independent and courageous, these spouses played their own crucial parts in the formation of the new republic.

MARTHA WASHINGTON

The First First Lady

A supportive partner, she helped guide her husband through the country's earliest days.

WHEN MARTHA DANDRIDGE CUSTIS MET George Washington, she was a wealthy young widow of 26 who had already lost a husband and two of her four children. Emotional hardship shaped her courageous outlook on life, but it never dimmed her cheerful nature. As she wrote to a friend after her husband was elected president, "I've learned from experience that the greater part of our happiness depends on our dispositions and not on our circumstances." Charming and attractive, she married the dashing military leader in 1759 and it was a true love match. In their early days together, they lived happily at his Virginia farm, Mount Vernon, where she helped manage the estate and raised her children (they had none of their own). When George was named to lead the Continental Army in the Revolutionary War, she accepted her new circumstances, though Washington wouldn't return home for eight years. Still, Washington's close friend, the Marquis de Lafayette, recalled the general sending for his wife during the cold winters, when the soldiers took a break from fighting. Martha was "a modest and respectable person who loves her husband madly," according to Lafayette, and she would make the treacherous journey to her husband's military camps throughout Pennsylvania and New Jersey. There, as the wife of

the commander in chief, she acted as his confidante and adviser, copying letters and representing him at official functions.

After the war, when George was nominated as the first president of the United States, Martha wasn't pleased, preferring the privacy of life at Mount Vernon. She complained to a friend, "I think it was much too late for him to go into public life again, but it was not to be avoided." Still, she dutifully moved with him to the nation's headquarters in New York, where the eyes of the public would be on them. Indeed, as first lady—a term not used until after her death—she graciously welcomed ordinary citizens, dignitaries

WEALTHY WIDOW By the time she wed George Washington on January 6, 1759 at age 27, Martha Dandridge Custis owned more than 17,500 acres of land—and enslaved nearly 300 people.

and members of Congress to the presidential home. When her husband declined to run for a third term in office, they returned to Mount Vernon, where they raised two of her four grandchildren as their own (her son had died in the Battle of Yorktown). After George died in 1799, she said, "Tis well…. All is over. I shall soon follow him! I have no more trials to pass through." She died three years later at age 70.

A LIFE OF LOSS
Martha gave birth to four children, all of whom she outlived. Neither her first son, Daniel, nor her first daughter, Frances, lived past age 5. Her daughter Patsy suffered severe seizures and died at age 17. And son John succumbed to a fever at age 27 after the Battle of Yorktown. Below, the first lady attends to Washington on his deathbed in 1799.

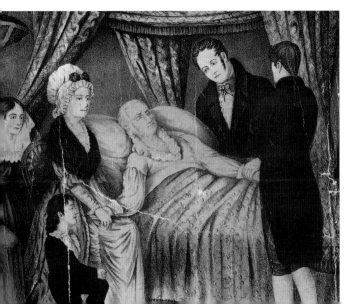

"The General and I feel like children just released from school or from a hard taskmaster, and we believe that nothing can tempt us to leave the sacred roof-tree again, except on private business or pleasure."

MARTHA WASHINGTON

DEAR JOHN
As John Adams' duties often kept him far from home, the couple relied on their frequent letters to each other to stay abreast of news, politics and life both at home and abroad.

ABIGAIL ADAMS
The Feminist Fighter

Intelligent, eloquent and willing to speak her mind, she was a source of strength and wisdom.

LONG BEFORE HILLARY AND BILL CLINTON aroused criticism as a Washington power couple with an opinionated female half, Abigail Adams faced precisely the same sort of scorn. "Mrs. President," her husband's opponents called her, mocking the closeness of her union with then-President John Adams. As was her custom, she shook the criticisms off and continued doing what she did throughout her remarkable 54-year marriage to one of America's most brilliant and opinionated presidents: expressing her own views with vehemence and grit. She could not have gone head-to-head with an intellect like John had she not been exceptionally intelligent and well-read herself—Abigail devoured every book she could get her hands on—and entirely secure in her right to share her thinking with those around her. At times in her role as first lady, however, Abigail wrestled with just how much to hold back her fervent views. "I have been so used to freedom of sentiment that I know nohow to place so many guards around me, as will be indispensable, to look at every word before I utter it and to impose a silence upon myself, when I long to talk," she reflected.

Abigail's road was not an easy one. With John frequently posted overseas, she was left to tend the couple's five children as well as manage the family farm on her own for a large portion of her marriage. She performed both tasks with exceptional grace, finding time in the process to participate in the exchange of more than 1,100 letters with John, a gift to posterity that offers an intimate profile of the era in which she lived, the issues of the day and the strength of her connection with the man she loved so deeply. Centuries before the modern feminist movement, she spoke up

FAMILY AFFAIRS Only one other woman—Barbara Bush— was both a first lady and mother to a president. Abigail would not live to see John Quincy Adams' election in 1824. Above, a statue of Abigail and John Quincy Adams.

for women. Understanding that economic dependency kept women restrained, "Remember the ladies," she wrote to John, "and be more generous and favorable to them than your ancestors. Do not put such unlimited power into the hands of the husbands. Remember all men would be tyrants if they could." Abigail died in 1818, just shy of her 74th birthday. Her last words were an expression of her love: "Do not grieve, my friend, my dearest friend. I am ready to go. And, John, it will not be long."

DOLLEY MADISON
The Fun-Loving Hostess

She brought light and laughter
to the White House, though her
final days ended darkly.

IF INSTAGRAM HAD BEEN ALIVE AND WELL IN 1809, hashtags like #WednesdayNightReception, #PartyWithDolley and #BuxomDame might very well be trending. Unlike her predecessors, Dolley Madison very much enjoyed her public role as the country's "first hostess."

Each Wednesday at the White House, Dolley held "drawing room" events that attracted politicians from both parties—a first for the often-divided elected officials. With her open-house policy, hundreds gathered to socialize, eat (yes, she served ice cream), amicably discuss policies, and enjoy music in the Red Room. Prior to her life in politics and Washington society, Dolley had dressed in the dull bonnets and drab dresses of her Quaker upbringing. Once she married her Episcopalian husband, James Madison, and left the faith, she embraced fashion trends that were—according to the accounts of several revelers of the day—as if she were playing the part of American royalty. Society and wealth had brought out her flair for the eccentric (see: ostrich feathers on a turban), prompting the nickname "Queen Dolley." But for all of the popular public glee that she was known for, Dolley was also loved by her peers for her warmth and intelligence.

Yet behind her upbeat public persona, Dolley had known tragedy: She suffered from the loss of both her first husband, John Todd, and her infant son to yellow fever. Payne Todd, her surviving son, was adopted and cared for by James, but he remained troubled throughout much of his adolescence. After James' death in 1836, Dolley placed the finances of their famed Montpelier plantation in her son's hands. Unfortunately, thanks to a combination of her extravagant spending and the mismanagement of the estate by her son, Payne (whose alcoholism left him with a string of debts), Dolley lived out her final years in financial ruin.

There was one boost to her income: Before her death, Dolley was able to sell James' papers and notes to Congress. Upon hearing that the House of Representatives had passed legislation to purchase the lot, the ever-charming Dolley said, "Oh Mr. Stephens! It was good of you to get my bill through today, but you made a very grave mistake when you said I was eighty-two today. I am not eighty-two: I am only eighty." She died in 1849 at the age of 81.

GOLD CHARM In 2007, the U.S. Mint issued its "first spouse" gold coin series in the order they served (Dolley Madison came fourth).

WEEPING WIDOW
Long after Alexander Hamilton lost his life in a duel, Eliza continued to mourn his loss. For years, she wore a small bag around her neck containing pieces of a sonnet he had composed for her.

ELIZABETH HAMILTON
The Steadfast Supporter

A widow for 50 years, she made it her mission to help others while honoring her husband's legacy.

LIN-MANUEL MIRANDA'S SMASH BROADway musical *Hamilton* summons a portrait of Elizabeth Hamilton, better known as Eliza, as both the privileged, educated and beautiful daughter of Revolutionary War Gen. Philip Schuyler as well as the suffering wife of Alexander Hamilton, destined to bear public humiliation with her husband's very public admission of adultery.

But there is so much more to Eliza's story, most of which was shaped in the 50 years after her husband was killed in the infamous duel with Aaron Burr. A mother of eight, as well as a foster mother to a Revolutionary War orphan, Eliza took up a philanthropic cause for the plight of orphans. (Alexander himself was orphaned at the age of 13.) She began her work with the Society for the Relief of Widows with Small Children, and in 1806, along with two other women, she co-founded New York City's first private orphanage, named the Orphan Asylum Society. She served twice as the Society's director, with her second stint ending at the spry age of 91.

Eliza was by all accounts a generous, intensely focused and compassionate problem solver. She was resolute in her mission to make education free and available to all children, and started a free public school in upper Manhattan so that children from Inwood and Washington Heights (near her uptown home, known as the Grange) would have access to education. But her family's own fortunes did not follow her, and she suffered her own financial woes after Alexander's death.

Despite her public marital difficulties, Eliza had forgiven Alexander and was deeply committed to preserving his reputation after his death, working fiercely and tirelessly to promote his legacy as a Founding Father. She gathered Alexander's writings and papers and was instrumental in the publishing of his biography in 1861, which traced the history of the birth of the country. Forever faithful, she wore a widow's black dress for the rest of her life. And by the time of her death, at age 97, her country celebrated her as a treasured link to America's revolutionary past, as well as a woman who envisioned hope for the future. Her extraordinary work continues over 200 years later. Eliza Hamilton's orphanage operates today as a family and youth development agency called Graham Windham, where it continues to create opportunities to help children and teens develop their own lasting legacies. ★

RESTING IN PEACE Eliza Hamilton is buried next to her husband at the Trinity Church graveyard in New York City; she was a dedicated parishioner there.

THE WHITE HOUSE

Seat of Power

As the nation's first president, George Washington selected the site for the White House, and after eight years of construction, John Adams and his wife, Abigail, moved in. Fellow Founding Fathers Thomas Jefferson, James Madison and James Monroe all subsequently took up residence in the building, which remains the place where executive policy is set, a powerful symbol of all the country has created and a family home. Here, a unique look inside the walls of the building today.

I. THE OVAL OFFICE
Established in its current location by President Franklin D. Roosevelt in 1933, the Oval Office is the president's primary work space and where he hosts the majority of his meetings.

2. THE CABINET ROOM
The vice president, secretary of state and more join the president around an oval mahogany table to discuss the issues of the day. The room overlooks the Rose Garden.

3. BLUE ROOM
Named for its all-blue decor, the Blue Room acts as a reception room for guests of the president. With a stunning view of the South Lawn, it makes for quite the first impression.

4. EAST ROOM
The largest room in the building, the East Room hosts major White House events. It is also often the site of private inaugurations for incoming presidents.

5. OFFICE OF THE FIRST LADY
The Office of the First Lady has moved several times and has evolved with the expectations of the role. Eleanor Roosevelt had two staffers; Hillary Clinton had 20.

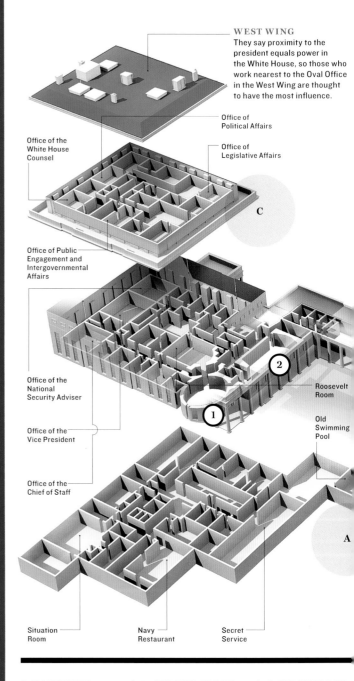

WEST WING
They say proximity to the president equals power in the White House, so those who work nearest to the Oval Office in the West Wing are thought to have the most influence.

Office of Political Affairs

Office of the White House Counsel

Office of Legislative Affairs

C

Office of Public Engagement and Intergovernmental Affairs

Office of the National Security Adviser

2

Roosevelt Room

Old Swimming Pool

Office of the Vice President

1

Office of the Chief of Staff

A

Situation Room

Navy Restaurant

Secret Service

A. BASEMENT
Sub-basement added during Truman Administration

B. GROUND FLOOR
Was known as the "basement" throughout the 1800s

C. FIRST FLOOR
Called the "State Floor" for its formal reception

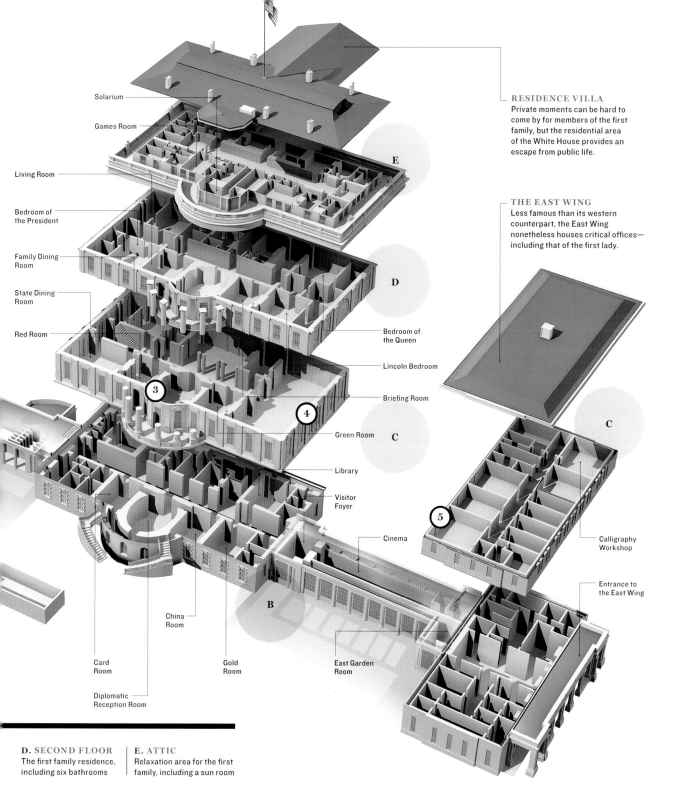

Solarium

Games Room

Living Room

Bedroom of
the President

Family Dining
Room

State Dining
Room

Red Room

E

D

C

B

Bedroom of
the Queen

Lincoln Bedroom

Briefing Room

Green Room

Library

Visitor
Foyer

Cinema

China
Room

Gold
Room

East Garden
Room

Card
Room

Diplomatic
Reception Room

RESIDENCE VILLA
Private moments can be hard to
come by for members of the first
family, but the residential area
of the White House provides an
escape from public life.

THE EAST WING
Less famous than its western
counterpart, the East Wing
nonetheless houses critical offices—
including that of the first lady.

C

Calligraphy
Workshop

Entrance to
the East Wing

D. SECOND FLOOR
The first family residence,
including six bathrooms

E. ATTIC
Relaxation area for the first
family, including a sun room

BY THE NUMBERS
Key Stats

55,000

SQUARE FEET ON
18 ACRES OF LAND

The White House property sits in a 77-acre area known as
President's Park, which also includes Lafayette Square,
The Ellipse and the White House Visitor Center.

3	**8**	**28**
ELEVATORS	STAIRCASES	FIREPLACES

35	**147**	**412**
BATHROOMS	WINDOWS	DOORS

...plus a bowling alley, movie theater, tennis court, putting green and more.

$232,372
ORIGINAL COST

$90M–$349M
RANGE OF ESTIMATES FOR VALUE TODAY

The historical value of the White House makes it impossible to put a price on, but that doesn't mean appraisal enthusiasts haven't tried. A 2016 estimate by real estate website Zillow appraised the building at a value of nearly $350 million.

570

GALLONS OF PAINT NEEDED TO COVER THE EXTERIOR

The paint color, made by Duron, is known as Whisper White.

5	96	250
FULL-TIME CHEFS	**FULL-TIME RESIDENCE STAFFERS**	**PART-TIME RESIDENCE STAFFERS**

White House staff is under the direction of the chief usher, helping to oversee the domestic life of the first family.

65,000

TOTAL OBJECTS IN THE ART COLLECTION

500

PAINTINGS IN THE ART COLLECTION

The first-ever piece acquired by the White House art collection was Gilbert Stuart's 1796 portrait of George Washington.

5,000

DAILY VISITORS

Requests for tours must be made at least 21 days in advance, so be sure to plan ahead.

A Nation Divided

Now is the time to overcome the Founding Fathers' worry that factionalism could spell the downfall of the American Experiment.

A S THIS BOOK IS PUBLISHED, America stands more bitterly divided than it's been since the Civil War. Even the angry diatribes of the 1960s could not rival the vitriol that passes for political discourse today. One source of the hostility is the internet, chock-full of unfiltered Twitter rants and one-sided blogs filled with false information and provocative conspiracy theories. Another is the rise of cable news, with its high-volume programs intended to stir their audiences on one end of the political spectrum or the other into a frenzy of self-righteous anger. A third is the diminishing influence of moderate voices in both political parties. But whatever the cause, the result is that we no longer simply disagree with the opinions of others; we actively despise the people holding them. Welcome to our world of hyperpartisanship.

What would the Founding Fathers think about the current state of our politics? Simply stated, they would be appalled. From the very beginning of their discussions about the future shape of the nation's government, the framers expressed their fear that the rise of political parties would produce a deeply destructive form of "factionalism." George Washington, the truly indispensable man in the early years of the republic,

agreed to serve a second term as president in part from a desire to hold in check the warring factions he saw emerging between those in favor of, and those opposed to, a strong federal government. And in his farewell address as he left office, he stated his views clearly: "The alternate domination of one faction over another, sharpened by the spirit of revenge, natural to party dissension, which in different ages and countries has perpetrated the most horrid enormities, is itself a frightful despotism." His fellow Founders felt similarly. Noted John Adams: "A division of the republic into two great parties...is to be dreaded as the great political evil." Alexander Hamilton described political parties as "the most fatal disease" of a democratic form of government. And James Madison argued that one of the key functions of government should be "its tendency to break and control the violence of faction."

What has led to today's deeply partisan environment? For much of American history, both major parties contained a diversity of political viewpoints. In the Republican Party, there was room for liberals like Nelson Rockefeller and John Lindsay of New York; the Democratic Party included conservatives like Joe Lieberman of Connecticut and Lloyd Bentsen of Texas. In a sense, America had four political parties, with distinct liberal (or moderate) wings of both parties vying for

influence with those further on the right or left. This diversity made political compromise not only possible but also commonplace, as alliances shifted within and between the parties. In those gentler times, the criticism, heard from liberals and conservatives alike, was that the two parties were too much alike, with the tendency to coalesce around the center, making our politics too timid, too prone to avoid the bold initiatives more ideological voters were seeking. But those moderate forces have all but disappeared today, and our two parties are now oceans apart on a wide array of fundamental questions about the direction of the country. Now, our parties represent not only differing ideologies, but conflicting cultures as well. Democrats are generally more urban, more ethnically diverse, more educated; Republican voters tend to be more exurban, more white and hold fewer advanced degrees. There are many exceptions to these demographics, of course, but together they represent distinctly differing world views on everything from where we get the news

EARLY PREDICTIONS In his farewell address, George Washington warned that fighting between political parties would divide the people and undermine the very foundations and principles of the United States.

(MSNBC or Fox News?), to the music we listen to (classical or country?), to the vehicles we drive (electric cars or pickup trucks?), and even to the foods we like to eat (barbecue or Asian fusion?).

The challenge of bridging this massive divide and finding common ground is enormous. President Joe Biden represents by any measure a more moderate point of view than his predecessor. But will anyone on the other side of the aisle listen? And can he persuade the progressive voices in his own party to

modulate their demands enough to achieve compromise with the opposition? Biden spent 36 years in the Senate representing the state of Delaware and has strong relationships with many current members, Republicans and Democrats alike. Will those connections prove effective in his search for new legislation on health care, climate change and infrastructure? The majority of U.S. presidents have been senators, vice presidents or governors before being elected to office. With Joe Biden having formerly held

two of these positions, he has a strong sense of what it takes to reach a compromise.

The notion of two intractably opposed political parties was anathema to the Founders; they would have preferred a multiparty system for America. Most advanced democracies today have at least three political parties, an arrangement that has sometimes produced chaos, but has also frequently forced compromise. Perhaps the time is ripe for a new political party (or two) in America, capable of breaking the current logjam and forcing our politicians—and ourselves—to listen to each another.

Absent that radical change, the best we can hope for is that a new generation of political leadership might emerge more attuned than those in office today to the common good and to the sentiments of our Founding Fathers. "There must be a positive Passion for the public good, the public Interest, Honor, Power, and Glory, established in the Minds

COMING TOGETHER The U.S. Capitol (top) is typically where Americans gather to celebrate the country's ideals, although it can also be the site of protest and discord. The Founding Fathers (right) are memorialized in the National Statuary Hall, along with many other leaders.

of the People," John Adams wrote, "or there can be no Republican Government, nor any real Liberty. And this public Passion must be Superior to all private Passions. Men must be ready, they must pride themselves, and be happy to sacrifice their private Pleasures, Passions, and Interests, nay their private Friendships and dearest connections, when they Stand in Competition with the Rights of society."

Here's hoping that passion for the public good still lingers in the soul of our nation, just waiting for the right moment to stake its claim on the hearts and minds of everyday Americans and their representatives in government. This would surely be the fervent wish of our Founding Fathers. We must not let them down. ★

N

National bank, 122–123
National Popular Vote Interstate Compact
    (NPVIC), 108
National Statuary Hall, 185
New York City
    British occupation of, 24–25
    Continental Army enters, 30
    map (1776), 113
New York Committee of Correspondence, 153
New York Manumission Society, 154
Ninth Amendment, 63, 65
NPVIC (National Popular Vote Interstate
    Compact), 108

O

Old State House, Boston, Massachusetts, 12, 42
Olive Branch Petition, 154
Opinion, single, Supreme Court rulings and, 158

P

Paine, Thomas, 12
Pennsylvania Gazette, 92, 94
Philadelphia, Pa.
    Constitutional Convention in, 54–57
    in early republic, 138–139
Political cartoon, first, 92
Popular vote, electoral college vs., 104–106, 109
Prescott, Samuel, 12
President, selection of, 102–109. *See also* Electoral
    College
Princeton, Battle of, 114–115
Princeton University, 135
"Probable cause," Bill of Rights and, 64
Publisher, Franklin as, 87–88, 92–93
Publius (pseudonym), 142

Q

Quartering Act (1765), 11
Quartering of soldiers, in Bill of Rights, 63, 65
Quill pens, 133

R

Racism, 7, 85. *See also* Slavery
Randolph, Edmund, 14, 57

Read, Deborah (wife of Franklin), 92, 94
Recolonization of the Americas, Monroe Doctrine
    and, 160
Religion
    freedom of worship and, 63, 65
    separation of church and state, 64–65
Revere, Paul
    engravings by, 40–43
    rides from Boston to Concord, 12, 131
Revolutionary War (1775-1783)
    American territories at time of, 27
    beginning of, 12, 28
    Madison in, 138, 140
    Treaty of Paris and, 13, 48, 101, 153, 154
    Washington's role in, 28–30
Rights
    enumeration of, in Bill of Rights, 63
    individual. *See* Individual rights
    states vs. federal, 144–151
Roosevelt, Theodore, 160
Royal Proclamation (1763), 8

S

Science experiments, of Franklin, 87, 91–92
Search and seizure of property, 63–64
Second Amendment, 63, 65
Second Continental Congress, 136
Senate, 62–63, 120
Separation of church and state, 64, 65
Seventh Amendment, 64–65
Shay's Rebellion, 13
Sherman, Roger, 32, 45, 57, 62–63, 72
Single opinion, Supreme Court rulings and, 158
Sixth Amendment, 64–65
Slave quarters, 84
Slave trade/ships, 85
Slavery, 82–85
    abolition of, 64
    Civil War and, 150
    numbers held under (1890 census), 82
    "three-fifths" compromise and, 85, 102, 104
Small, William, 68
Sons of Liberty, 7, 130
Southern states, "three-fifths" compromise and,
    85, 102, 105

SPECIAL THANKS TO CONTRIBUTING WRITER

Theresa Gambacorta

CENTENNIAL BOOKS

An Imprint of
Centennial Media, LLC
40 Worth St., 10th Floor
New York, NY 10013, U.S.A.

ISBN 978-1-951274-67-2

Distributed by
Simon & Schuster, Inc.
1230 Avenue of the Americas
New York, NY 10020, U.S.A.

For information about custom editions, special sales and premium and corporate purchases, please contact Centennial Media at contact@centennialmedia.com.

Manufactured in Singapore

PUBLISHERS & CO-FOUNDERS Ben Harris, Sebastian Raatz
EDITORIAL DIRECTOR Annabel Vered
CREATIVE DIRECTOR Jessica Power
EXECUTIVE EDITOR Janet Giovanelli
FEATURES EDITOR Alyssa Shaffer
DEPUTY EDITORS Ron Kelly, Anne Marie O'Connor
MANAGING EDITOR Lisa Chambers
DESIGN DIRECTOR Martin Elfers
SENIOR ART DIRECTOR Pino Impastato
ART DIRECTORS Runyon Hall, Natali Suasnavas, Joseph Ulatowski
COPY/PRODUCTION Patty Carroll, Angela Taormina
ASSISTANT ART DIRECTOR Jaclyn Loney
SENIOR PHOTO EDITOR Jenny Veiga
PHOTO EDITOR Keri Pruett
PRODUCTION MANAGER Paul Rodina
PRODUCTION ASSISTANT Alyssa Swiderski
EDITORIAL ASSISTANT Tiana Schippa
SALES & MARKETING Jeremy Nurnberg